Introduction to child development

Introduction to child development

Patricia Hicks

Tutor, Thomas Danby College, Leeds

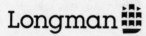

LONGMAN GROUP LIMITED
Longman House, Burnt Mill,
Harlow, Essex CM20 2JE, England
and Associated Companies throughout the World.

First published 1981
Third impression 1984

ISBN 0 582 36149 4

Cataloguing in Publication Data

Hicks, Patricia
    Introduction to child development.
    (Longman early childhood education; no. 6)
    1. Child psychology
    2. Child development
    I. Title
    155.4′22   BF721
    ISBN 0-582-36149-4

Printed in Hong Kong by
Wilture Printing Co. Ltd.

ACKNOWLEDGEMENTS

I acknowledge, with sincere thanks, the help and encouragement of
my colleagues, Michelle Pashley and David Pugh.

Cover photograph: Colin Maher

To Miss Isabell Briggs, whose professional life was devoted to so many children.

Foreword

This book is the outcome of observing the difficulties that Nursery Nurse students experience in studying normal child development. Too often, students attempt to learn by rote a timetable of children's performance at certain ages. Then learning becomes boring and the children they meet rarely conform to expectations.

Each child is unique, often requiring intuitive management by the caring adult. Intuition being a rare quality, the best aid a student can possess is a sound knowledge of how children grow and develop. It follows, therefore, that the learning of this fascinating subject should be enjoyed.

I have attempted to offer an alternative method of studying children, emphasising patterns of child development.

Throughout the book, the child is referred to as 'he' and the teacher/playgroup leader as 'she'; this is purely for convenience.

Contents

1
Growth and development

The full term baby enters this world completely dependent upon adults for his means of survival. The baby's only built-in protection is the collection of reflexes, some permanent lasting a lifetime and some temporary ones, which accommodate a need until **maturity** brings voluntary controlled action. Maturity is brought about through two processes:

1 *Growth* – increase in size
2 *Development* – increase in complexity i.e. a qualitative change bringing improvement in function or performance.

These processes are dynamic, continuous and, in some cases, irregular in tempo. Individual parts of the body mature at individual rates e.g. the brain is well developed at birth but its subsequent performance will improve more rapidly in the first few years of life than, say, the reproductive organs which lie dormant until the onset of puberty. It is, to some extent, a question of priorities and Nature is an expert at determining the order of those priorities. Those organs which are an obvious necessity to the maintenance of life are sufficiently proficient to support that life. Others become proficient in good time, as the needs of the child dictate e.g. the skeletal and muscular systems.

Each child grows and develops in his own particular way, but when large numbers of children are studied a pattern emerges which, for ease of assessment, we accept as the normal progress. It is 'normal' for the body, personality and intellect to develop in harmony.

PRINCIPLES OF DEVELOPMENT

1 Development is a continuous process
From **conception** to maturity, the developing child is changing. The changes taking place are fluid and continuous, although the tempo is erratic. During foetal life and infancy, growth is at its

Fig 1.1

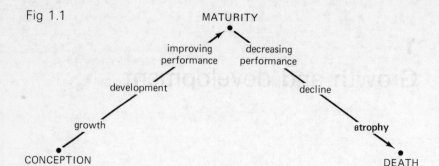

most rapid, deceleration occurs in childhood, with a rapid acceleration in **adolescence**. As long as these fits and starts are recognised for what they are, no harm is done.

It seems as if two major skills cannot be learned at the same time. This is demonstrated clearly in the child of about 1 year old who has acquired a vocabulary of 3–5 words and is learning to walk at the same time. The excitement caused by the acquisition of this new skill of mobility, and the opportunities which present themselves as a result, may detract from language skill, which slows temporarily. As soon as the child becomes completely confident in large motor skills they no longer require his intense concentration and language development goes ahead.

This pattern is repeated in later life, during adolescence. Rapid increase in height, weight and physical maturity may result in a temporary neglect of school academic work. Over anxious parents and teachers who lack understanding may delay what might otherwise be a smooth passage through a temporary, if significant, phase.

An awareness of this continuous process avoids division of development into 'milestones'. Milestones provide a useful professional shorthand, but emphasis on them in terms of the age at which a skill is achieved can cause great anxiety and give rise to very limited observation of *one* area of development. We must never depart from assessment of the whole child and the performance of new skills must be seen in relation to overall development.

2 Development depends upon maturation of the nervous system

No amount of practice will make a child learn a particular skill if his nervous system is not sufficiently developed to control it. Once this voluntary control has occurred, the opportunity for practice must be given. When practice is denied, the skill lies dormant. This principle applies to much of our care of children;

an obvious example being the management of hygiene habits and 'potty practice' (see Chapter 8).

Discovery of the presence of a skill should be followed by practice and reinforced by adult approval. Each new skill developed must be a rewarding experience if it is to be repeated and ultimately perfected within the potential of the individual.

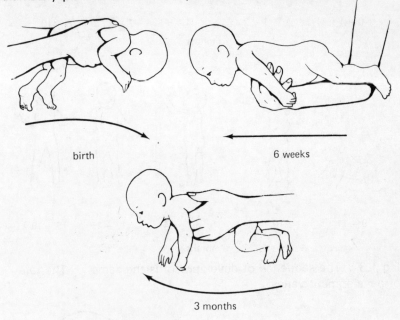

birth   6 weeks

3 months

Fig 1.2 **ventral suspension**—nervous maturation

3 Development sequence
The sequence of development is the same for all children. The *rate* of development varies from child to child. For example, most children sit alone before they walk. The age at which a child sits alone varies from 6 to 10 months; walking alone can vary from 12 to 20 months (see Figure 1.3).

4 Reflex and voluntary actions
Some **reflex actions** must be lost in order that voluntary actions may develop. Certain primitive reflexes are present at birth. Some are protective and remain with us during our lifetime e.g. blinking, sneezing and coughing. Others accommodate a temporary need and will be lost, indeed must be lost, before the voluntary action develops e.g. grasping, walking and the reciprocal kick.

Poorly developed reflexes would lead one to suspect a degree of immaturity in the baby. Prolonged presence of these poorly developed reflexes may indicate mental retardation. It is not

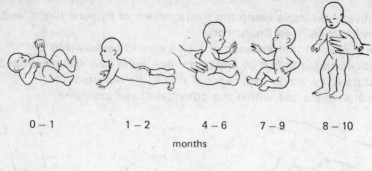

0 – 1   1 – 2   4 – 6   7 – 9   8 – 10

months

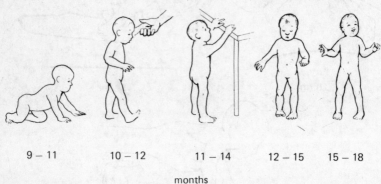

9 – 11   10 – 12   11 – 14   12 – 15   15 – 18

months

Fig 1.3   'The sequence of development is the same ... The *rate* of development varies ...'

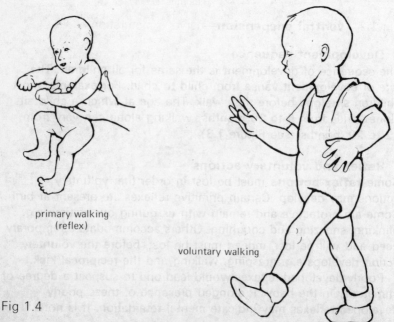

primary walking
(reflex)

voluntary walking

Fig 1.4

4

uncommon to find grasp and walking reflexes in mentally handicapped children of 3 years or more. Normally the grasp reflex would go away around 3–4 months, ready for the voluntary grasp to develop; the primitive walking reflex should not be observed after the 6th–8th week of life.

5 Developmental directions

The directions of development are cephalocaudal and proximodistal. These terms are defined as follows:

'cephalo' – head; 'caudal' – tail,

that is, the direction that development takes is downwards from head to tail;

'proximal' – near to the mid-line; 'distal' – far from the mid-line,

that is, development progresses from the mid-line to the extremities. Development progresses simultaneously in this way.

Head control, eye focusing and social expression come before sitting, reaching and social babbling. Control of the upper arm, the ability to stretch the arm, comes before crude grasping with the whole hand. The very refined pincer grasp using thumb and forefinger develops even later.

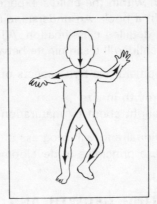

Fig 1.5
cephalocaudal
and proximodistal

6 Replacement of general body activity

General body activity in response to emotional stimulation is replaced by a specific action. If we observe the demonstration of pleasure in different age groups we see this principle clearly.

The baby expresses **emotion** with his whole body. Pleasure is expressed by a wide smile, bright eyes, aimless movements of arms and legs, a raised respiration and heart rate. Imagine the small girl of 5 years of age on Christmas morning. A bright smile, exclamations of delight, tensed hands, perhaps a jump or a skip.

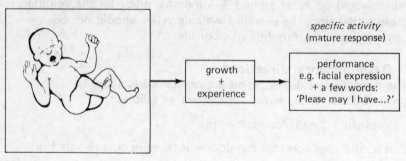

generalised activity
(immature response)

specific activity
(mature response)

growth
+
experience

performance
e.g. facial expression
+ a few words:
'Please may I have...?'

Fig 1.6

These signs leave us in no doubt of her excitement and pleasure. She still uses body movements as a means of communication, but she has now developed language and can express herself verbally.

If we follow this development to maturity we notice that the adult expresses delight by facial expression and a few significant words. The response has changed from whole body activity to a simple specific response. Similarly, in **concept formation**, the child will progress from the general to the specific. 'Daddy' will often mean every man within the child's experience, whether he is a visitor or a picture in a book. An understanding of groups or sets will come before detailed classification. All animals may be 'dog'. Much later the child will discriminate between the species.

To summarise, development has two aspects of change:

a) one of quantity, growth in size
b) one of quality, brought about by maturation.

Each child is an individual and will progress at his own rate, but conforming to these principles of development.

FACTORS AFFECTING GROWTH AND DEVELOPMENT
The **factors** that affect growth and development can be grouped into 3 distinct classes:

pre-natal
Any influence coming to bear on the child prior to the onset of labour.

peri-natal
The conditions pertaining at delivery and the method of delivery.

post-natal
The plethora of factors that will influence the child on entering this world and for the rest of his life.

Pre-natal factors affecting growth and development

1 Heredity
The characteristics endowed to the child by his parents and other ancestors.

It is common that a child inherits many of the characteristics of both mother and father. These characteristics are passed to the child by means of filaments known as **chromosomes**, which are found in the **nucleus** of any cell. Arranged in linear sequence along the chromosomes are small substances called **genes**. Each gene has its particular place in the chain and its particular function in inheritance. They form the 'recipe' for that particular individual. Every species has a prescribed number of chromosomes. The normal human being has 23 pairs of chromosomes. Each parent contributes half of this number to the offspring. Each mature sperm and each mature ovum contains 23 single chromosomes. When these two cells unite at conception, the 'ingredients' of 23 pairs are provided for the new being which will develop.

When the chromosomes unite, the genes are paired i.e. every gene in one of a pair of chromosomes is paired with a gene in another chromosome. If the paired genes are similar in their performance, the characteristics which they influence will appear in the child. If they are dissimilar, their different effects may combine to produce a slightly altered characteristic or one gene may dominate the other and is said to be 'dominant'. The **recessive gene** will remain and may be evident in a later generation. This explains why certain characteristics will 'skip a generation'.

To complicate the issue further, some characteristics may be linked to the sex of the individual and are termed sex-linked characteristics. Examples of these are **haemophilia** and **colour blindness**, which are prevalent in boys. The characteristic is carried on the 'X' chromosome and may therefore be carried by the female and transmitted to her offspring.

Whilst the number of chromosomes donated by each parent is usually 23, each resulting in 23 pairs in the developing child, the grouping of these chromosomes is largely a matter of chance and explains why one child in a family strongly resembles his mother whilst another resembles his father. Occasionally, a new trait appears in a family, due to a process known as **mutation.** This results due to a change in the original gene and is rarely for the better. A modern cause of mutation is the effect of **radiation** upon the genes.

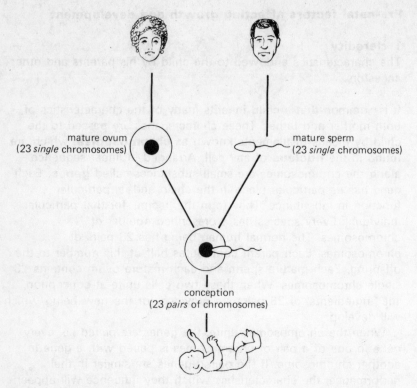

Fig 1.7   genetic inheritance

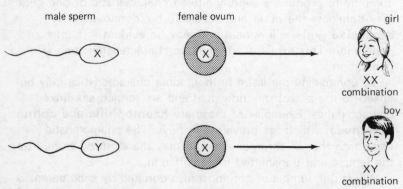

Fig 1.8   sex determination

One of the parents is bound to transmit his or her sex to the offspring. Among the 23 pairs of chromosomes, one pair is especially concerned with determination of sex. In the female, this particular pair is equal in size and similar in composition – the **X** chromosomes. In the male, one of the pair is an X chromosome, the other is smaller and known as the **Y** chromosome. As the male sperms develop to full maturity, division occurs resulting in half the sperms containing X chromosomes and the other half containing Y chromosomes. If the female ovum is fertilised by a sperm containing an X chromosome the two X chromosomes pair off and a female child will develop. If the female ovum is fertilised by a sperm containing a Y chromosome the XY combination will result in a male child.

2 Conditions in the womb
When one or more babies are developing at the same time, the presence of **fibroids**, or any abnormality in the structure of the uterus, may adversely affect the developing child.

Twin pregnancy
The incidence of twins is approximately 1:80 i.e. 1 in every 80 pregnancies is a twin pregnancy. Twins can occur in one of two ways.

In some cases the fertilised ovum divides into 2, and 2 separate embryos develop; each with its own **umbilical cord** and bag of membranes, but sharing a common **placenta**. These are uniovular or identical twins. Identical because they have developed from the same sperm, the same ovum and therefore their hereditary endowment is the same. The children will be of the same sex and be similar in appearance and temperament although size is often different initially. Since both depend upon the same placenta for their survival, one may be 'greedier' than the other and develop at the expense of the other.

Binovular or fraternal twins result from 2 eggs which are fertilised simultaneously by 2 separate sperms. As a result, they are only as alike as any 2 brothers, 2 sisters, or brother and sister, but they happened to share the same period of pregnancy. Each has his own placenta, bag of membranes and umbilical cord.

During pregnancy, twins are more likely to be miscarried or delivered prematurely. Birth difficulties are also more common with twins and may result in birth injuries.

Twin pregnancy is more common with parents who have a family history of twins.

Characteristics of twins
Many people are interested in the physical and mental similarities of twins. These are often cause for astonishment and occasionally confusion but, at a deeper level, twins do seem to have problems just because they are twins. Language development can be delayed. This may be explained by the fact that any 2 children in the early stages of language development will evolve their own 'scribble talk' which is apparently understood by them alone.

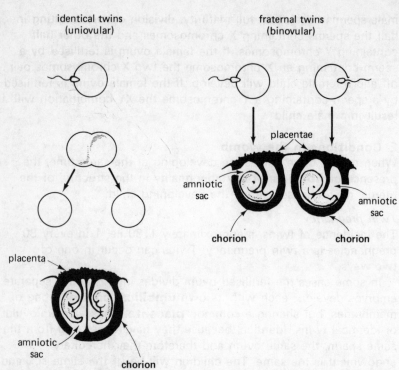

identical twins
(uniovular)

fraternal twins
(binovular)

placentae

amniotic
sac

amniotic
sac

chorion

chorion

placenta

amniotic
sac

chorion

Fig 1.9   types of twins

Communication by gesture and an apparent thought reading ability obviates the need for the spoken word. This is heightened with twins who spend much of their time together. Their social development is almost certain to be affected for good or ill by the constant closeness of a playmate of the same age. This could help them to make relationships more easily. Conversely, they may become so dependent upon each other that they exclude others from their very private relationship.

The most significant effect of being a twin is that the close mother/child relationship is shared right from the beginning. Twins will obviously be more demanding on the time, skill, patience and love of the mother figure and this may predispose to an early close relationship being formed with another adult, often father.

How difficult it can be for the twin to develop his own personality and identity. Frequently we hear twins referred to as 'the twins' and seldom by name. Often they are regarded as 1 being rather than 2 developing individuals. Perhaps this indicates that twins are at risk of deprivation in some areas of their development and the caring adult should attempt to avoid the obvious pitfalls in their management.

Triplets
Triplets can arise in one of the following ways:

- 3 babies which develop from the same sperm and ovum, as identical twins
- 1 set of identical twins and a third child
- 3 quite separate fertilised ova.

Multiple pregnancies
Occasionally, as a result of hormone therapy for infertility, a woman may carry many babies at one time. Such babies are usually well below the average birth weight and greatly at risk of miscarriage in pregnancy or of non-survival at birth.

Siamese or conjoined twins
This rare condition occurs due to the incomplete division of uniovular twins. Obviously, delivery is hazardous, but a greater threat to survival is determined by the point of junction and what internal organs are shared. Successful separation has been achieved by surgical operation.

3 Blood groups and Rhesus incompatibility
It is beyond the scope of this book to examine in detail blood groups and the Rhesus factor. However, no book on child development would be complete without reference to these topics.

There are four main blood types: A, B, AB and O. Blood type is another hereditary characteristic conferred on the child by the parents. In addition, there is a substance found in the blood of some humans which is known as the Rhesus Factor. This name is derived from the fact that this substance is also present in the blood of the Rhesus monkey. On average, 85% of human beings possess this factor and are said to be Rhesus positive (Rh+), the remaining 15% who do not possess this substance are considered Rhesus negative (Rh−).

A baby inherits two Rhesus genes, one from each parent, and the Rhesus positive (D) gene is dominant. If both parents are Rhesus negative (dd) the baby will be dd also. If one parent is DD and the other dd, he will be Dd (positive). If one parent is Dd and the other dd, the baby may be Dd (positive) or dd (negative).

As part of her ante-natal care ('ante' − before; 'natal' − birth), the mother's blood will be classified or 'typed' according to blood group and the presence or absence of the Rhesus factor will be determined. If she is Rhesus positive, the baby is not at risk. If she is Rhesus negative, regular samples of blood will be examined to assess any potential danger to her child, who may be Rhesus

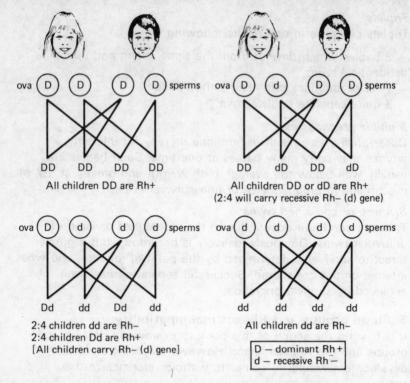

ova (D) (D) (D) (D) sperms   ova (D) (d) (D) (D) sperms

DD   DD   DD   DD   DD   dD   DD   dD
All children DD are Rh+   All children DD or dD are Rh+
                                 (2:4 will carry recessive Rh- (d) gene)

ova (D) (d) (d) (d) sperms   ova (d) (d) (d) (d) sperms

Dd   dd   Dd   dd   dd   dd   dd   dd
2:4 children dd are Rh-   All children dd are Rh-
2:4 children Dd are Rh+
[All children carry Rh- (d) gene]

| D - dominant Rh + |
| d - recessive Rh - |

Fig 1.10   inheritance of Rhesus factor, showing possible combinations at fertilisation

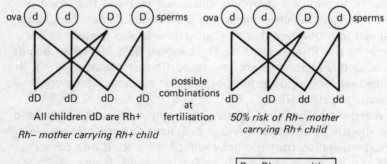

ova (d) (d) (D) (D) sperms   ova (d) (d) (D) (d) sperms

                                          possible
                                          combinations
                                          at
dD   dD   dD   dD   fertilisation   dD   dD   dd   dd
All children dD are Rh+   50% risk of Rh- mother
                                               carrying Rh+ child
Rh- mother carrying Rh+ child

| D - Rhesus positive |
| d - Rhesus negative |

Fig 1.11   Rhesus incompatibility

positive. If the mother is Rhesus negative and the baby is Rhesus positive, she may react to this foreign substance in her baby's blood and make **antibodies** to attack and destroy the foreign cells. This is called Rhesus incompatibility.

The risk is minimal with the first pregnancy, but at delivery of this child, when the placenta separates, some of the baby's blood cells may pass into the mother's blood stream, causing her to make a considerable amount of antibodies which will be retained in the mother's body. She herself will feel no ill effects, but these antibodies will pass to the baby in subsequent pregnancies. The amount of damage done to the child can vary from mild **anaemia** to **jaundice**, to brain damage or even cause death (Rhesus Haemolytic Disease of the newborn).

A baby suffering from a mild anaemia can be simply treated with iron. A child who is severely jaundiced and in danger of brain damage may require an exchange transfusion. This title is misleading, since it implies that all the baby's blood is exchanged for fresh blood. In fact, small quantities of the baby's destroyed blood are withdrawn and replaced by wholesome blood to dilute the jaundice to a safe level. This procedure is performed soon after birth, using a blood vessel in the umbilical cord. This is a very effective treatment, but one that may need to be repeated. Often follow-up treatment with a little extra iron is all that is required.

Early inducement of labour and the delivery of a pre-term infant may be considered desirable when the antibody formation is excessive and the child's life is at risk. A recent alternative, which has become available due to improved scanning techniques, is intra-uterine transfusion. The child is transfused whilst still in the uterus in the hope that life is maintained until the child is mature enough to be born.

As a preventive measure, a sample of the Rhesus negative mother's blood is taken immediately following delivery of the first child and examined for the presence of foetal blood cells. If necessary she will then be given an injection of Anti-D gamma globulin which will prevent antibody formation and ensure the safety of subsequent children.

4 Maternal ill health

Pregnant women are no more and no less likely to suffer infectious diseases than others. However, if infection is contacted special care is taken of the woman in order to protect her unborn child who is not totally protected by the placenta. Some infections, particularly those of viral origin, pass across the 'barrier' of the placenta and can harm the child's development or predispose to **abortion** or **prematurity**.

Of particular importance are the **venereal diseases**. By virtue of being pregnant the woman, any woman, is at risk of infection passed during sexual intercourse and, because of this, screening for venereal diseases, especially **gonorrhoea** and **syphilis**, is carried out in the ante-natal period. (Screening is a word used to describe the large scale investigation of people who may be at risk of a particular condition.) This investigation is usually carried out after obtaining a blood sample taken from the woman at her first ante-natal clinic visit. Any infection discovered is treated and provided treatment is started early on in the pregnancy there is little risk of harm to the child.

Untreated gonorrhoea in the mother can result in a very dangerous eye condition occurring in the child. Untreated syphilis in the mother could give rise to a stillborn infant.

Maternal Rubella (German measles) in the first 3–4 months of pregnancy can result in nerve damage or congenital heart defect in the baby. It is desirable, therefore, that the pregnant woman should avoid contacting Rubella.

Due to the demands made by the developing **foetus** on the store of iron in the woman's body, it is necessary to ensure that anaemia does not develop. This could ultimately result in depletion of the supply of iron to the child. The foetus of a **diabetic** mother tends to grow very large, which may complicate delivery. Despite good management there is still a relatively high infant mortality rate associated with diabetes in the mother.

The mental health of the mother is of great importance. It is believed by some **paediatricians** that a mentally stable mother is a pre-requisite for a mentally stable child. It is not uncommon for **depression** to occur in pregnancy, but is more common soon after delivery. The causes of depression in pregnancy can be many and varied: poverty, marital disharmony, too many children too quickly, illegitimate or unplanned pregnancy, are some of the common causes and may ultimately culminate in a depression which requires medical care. Our Social Services are attempting, more and more, to alleviate or remove such difficulties. Voluntary organisations as well as general practitioners and health visitors are advising those couples who seek advice regarding planned parenthood.

Toxaemia of pregnancy is relatively common and only presents a hazard to the child if it is unchecked. Toxaemia is the medical word for the presence of toxins or poisons circulating in the blood. This does not indicate a state of infection, rather a situation demonstrating that the woman's body is reacting to the physical stresses imposed upon it by the baby's presence. The condition is alleviated by delivery and the woman usually makes a spontaneous recovery.

Unchecked, or in severe form, toxaemia can result in the premature delivery of the child. This is usually an induced delivery, brought on under medical supervision in order to protect the health of the mother. The child may then have to overcome the disadvantages of prematurity.

5 Drugs
Any drug is potentially poisonous. At least, it is a foreign chemical substance introduced into the body to bring about changes. Whilst the drug itself is prescribed for the benefit of the mother, many prescriptions create a vulnerable situation for the baby. There have been examples of drugs, given to alleviate excessive vomiting, causing physical abnormality in the baby. These are most unfortunate accidents. Worse are the cases of drug-addicted babies born to mothers who themselves are addicts.

6 Cigarette smoking
This undesirable habit has dangerous implications for the health of both mother and child. It has been demonstrated that the unusually low birth weight of full term infants delivered by women who indulge in excessive cigarette smoking is not coincidental. There is evidence to suggest that some miscarriages may be attributed to this habit. Carbon monoxide inhaled in cigarette smoke inhibits the oxygen take-up by the red blood cells, thereby diminishing the supply of oxygen for the child.

7 Diet
Since the mother must provide for the nutritious needs of her child, the importance of a high quality diet in pregnancy must be stressed. Reference to the need for iron has already been made, but it is equally important that all food groups are taken in correctly balanced amounts in order to provide for the child and bring the mother to her confinement healthy and fit to cope with the hard work of labour.

8 The duration of pregnancy
The full term of pregnancy is 40 weeks. A child born at full term is better equipped for the strains of delivery and the demands of life than the premature child. Similarly, postmaturity brings with it certain problems.

9 Radiation
Brief mention of radiation was made in connection with mutation. There are 4 chief sources of radiation to which we are exposed in varying amounts at different times of life: cosmic rays; X-rays used for diagnosis and treatment; radiation released in the production and use of atomic energy; and the escape of radiation from naturally occurring radioactive material.

Protection lies in the controls on radioactive material and in particular the care taken to avoid exposing pregnant women to X-rays except in great necessity. Men and women working in potentially dangerous occupations e.g. radiography wear small devices which measure the amount of radiation to which they are exposed.

Peri-natal factors affecting growth and development

With the improvement in ante-natal care, the special training of nurses, midwives and health visitors and an improvement in the health of women generally, many of the risks attached to delivery have been overcome or alleviated. Infant and maternal mortality rates have dropped accordingly in the more sophisticated countries.

However, it is impossible to remove all the hazards of delivery which is in every case unpredictable in its progress. Adverse conditions at delivery include the following:

a) foetal distress, usually due to a temporary lack of oxygen (anoxia), may necessitate speeding up the delivery by an assisted or **forceps delivery**, **Ventouse extraction** or **Caesarian section**. (Caesarian section is performed either as an emergency procedure as in the case above, or as an elective procedure which means the **obstetrician** diagnosed an abnormality in pregnancy and took the decision before the woman went into labour.)

b) if a general anaesthetic is administered for delivery the baby is exposed to the anaesthetic and may need resuscitation following delivery.

c) a **breech presentation** or other abnormal birth can prolong the labour and result in a fatigued mother and an anoxic or shocked baby. The danger of anoxia is primarily one of brain damage. The brain cells, if depleted of oxygen for even a short time, can be irreparably damaged and depending upon the degree of anoxia may result in a range of disorders from minimal brain damage to severe abnormality.

Post-natal factors affecting growth and development

1 Environment

This all enveloping word is used to describe our total surroundings, including the family, the community and country in which that family lives. Whilst heredity decides the amount of potential endowed to the child, the environment determines the limits to which that potential develops.

The family structure is one of the strongest influences. For example, is this a 1 or 2 parent family? What are their ages? How many children are there already? What is the age difference between them? What position will the new arrival have? Are more children hoped for?

Many families are capable of economic dependence if one or both parents are in regular employment. Some find 2 incomes an absolute necessity and others require financial help from the State to function effectively. The future of a child born into each of these situations will obviously be affected for good or ill by the circumstances found there (see Chapter 10, section on *The family*).

2 Personal and communal hygiene

Hygiene is defined as the study of measures necessary to promote health. This subject will therefore cover the 'mental, physical and social wellbeing' (World Health Organisation definition of health) of the child. It must include nutrition, sleep and rest, fresh air and exposure to sunlight, exercise, safety, protection against infection, personal and communal cleanliness, positive mental health and constructive use of leisure.

3 Hormones

Hormones are very powerful chemical substances which are made by glands known as the endocrine glands. From the place of manufacture, a hormone is passed directly into the blood stream and thereby circulated to those parts of the body where it has a specific function to perform. These functions vary, from influencing the rate of growth and maturation to regulating emotional responses. Often there is an interlocking of the functions of two glands which results in them working together to achieve a common purpose.

Hormone production is determined, to a large extent, by hereditary influences.

The thyroid gland

This gland is situated in the neck. Its hormone affects the rate of general growth, bone development, the nervous system, muscle development, circulation and function of the reproductive organs.

A severe lack of the thyroid hormone before birth gives rise to cretinism. This one word describes a child whose overall growth is retarded, who is mentally deficient, who is slow and clumsy in movement and whose tongue is typically large and protruding.

A cretin commonly has an umbilical **hernia**. This is so common that it is fair to say almost all cretins have an umbilical hernia *but* it does not follow that all children with umbilical herniae are cretins.

Without treatment, the child would be a sort of Peter Pan – the eternal child in physical appearance and intellect. If the condition is recognised and treated early, there is every possibility that normal standards of development will be achieved.

The parathyroid glands

The four parathyroid glands lie two on either side of the thyroid gland. Despite this closeness, they have their own specific function of controlling the use in the body of calcium and phosphorus. These two minerals are vital for healthy bones and teeth, efficient muscle action (particularly the action of the heart) and the clotting of the blood.

Irregular production of this hormone is rarely seen in children. However, too little may result in tetany, a condition causing painful muscle cramps. Too much parathyroid hormone can cause softening of the bones and weak muscle activity.

The pancreas

This is a gland situated in the abdomen, below the stomach and having two functions:

a) production of a substance which is necessary for proper digestion of some foods
b) production of insulin which regulates the use of sugar in the body.

The first of these, an **enzyme**, can be diminished in supply if a child suffers from **cystic fibrosis**, a condition which is attracting much attention. The digestive disturbances which follow must be controlled by diet and synthetic enzyme treatment.

Irregularity in the amount of insulin liberated leads to a condition known as diabetes mellitus (sugar diabetes). This condition can be controlled by special diet and/or the injection of regulated doses of insulin. Treatment by tablets taken orally is also available in some cases, *but never for children*.

It is important to note that every diabetic is a unique case. Each requires careful diagnosis, physiological measurement and treatment for his/her particular needs.

The adrenal glands

These glands sit like hats on top of the kidneys. Like the pancreas, these glands have more than one function. One is concerned with the control of some mineral substances in the body and therefore affects growth. Another has an important role to play in sexual maturity and really becomes active at around 9 or 10 years in preparation for the onset of puberty. A third, adrenalin, is known as the 'fight or flight' hormone. This enables the body to cope with sudden stress. Due to its action the body is prepared for vigorous activity during fear, anger or emotional upset. We become capable of standing up and 'fighting' the cause of stress or we gain the extra energy needed for 'flight'. An example here is the way in which a person will vault a gate if confronted by an angry bull; a feat which might be impossible in times of calm.

The testes and ovaries
The reproductive glands are the testes in the male and the ovaries in the female. Each produces the cell which will enable the individual to reproduce. They are also concerned with the production of the male or female hormones which bring about the changes of adolescence; those changes which turn a girl into a mature woman capable of bearing children and a boy into a mature man capable of producing mature sperms.

The pituitary gland
The pituitary gland is described as 'the leader of the endocrine orchestra'. It is a very small structure, situated at the base of the brain.

Deficiency of pituitary function can cause pituitary dwarfism. The person has proportions which compare with his age, but his features remain very childish and he seldom reaches sexual maturity. The intelligence is usually unaffected.

As previously stated, it is normal for all sections of the body and mind to work in harmony. No single part can operate without the support of other structures or systems. In no other system is this seen more clearly than in the effects of endocrine activity on wholesome growth and healthy personality development.

4 Infection
Several childhood infections can significantly affect growth and development. Some of the more serious ones, **poliomyelitis**, **tuberculosis**, **whooping cough** etc, can be controlled by a suitable immunisation programme. For the first few weeks of life a baby is protected to some degree by natural immunity gained from the mother in utero and enhanced by antibodies gained from breast feeding. Otherwise, the child is dependent upon the development of his own immunity responses. These include the thymus gland, the **tonsils** and **adenoids**, white cells in the blood and the increasing store of antibodies and antitoxins that he makes in response to contact with infection.

The thymus gland
This gland lies in the upper chest, behind the breast bone. The thymus gland, and specifically thymic hormone, helps in the formation of antibodies and **lymphocytes**. It has an important protective function in childhood when it is extremely large in proportion to chest size. Soon after puberty, it begins to shrink and is barely visible in adults.

Tonsils and adenoids
The tonsils and adenoids are other important areas of lymphatic tissue which help to protect the child from infection. Like the thymus gland, both the tonsils and the adenoids are excessively large in childhood and regress as the child's other immunity responses become efficient. They are the first line of defence to respiratory tract infection. Sometimes, due to repeated attacks of infection the tonsils and/or adenoids become so damaged that regression is delayed and they themselves become a source of infection. In such a case, it may be in the child's best interests to remove them.

White blood cells
White blood cells also have an important part to play in protection from infection. The white cell count at birth is relatively high and later falls. White cell count rises whenever a state of infection exists.

Exposure to infection is an unavoidable facet of life. It is a risk which must be minimised by maintenance of good health, sensible precautions and protection of the most vulnerable.

BASIC NEEDS OF ALL CHILDREN
Due to the complexity of the human being, the developing and maturing process takes longer than any other animal. The period of dependency on adults, therefore, is also longer. During this time, every child has basic needs which must be met if he is to complete the maturation process successfully:

1 implementation of the principles of health — nutrition, sleep, rest, exercise, cleanliness, warmth, security, protection against infection, injury and harmful emotional experience

2 continuity of affection and care

3 suitable materials and experiences which ensure foundations for physical, social, emotional, intellectual, moral and aesthetic development

4 communication through physical contact, gesture, facial expression and speech

5 a satisfactory model for learning social skills

6 freedom, opportunity and encouragement to acquire independence safely.

2
Conception to birth

Pregnancy is the period of 40 weeks during which the mother harbours and nourishes the developing child. It is a function for which a woman is physically designed, but one which needs skilled supervision if it is to proceed successfully. Childbearing puts a strain on a woman's body and may exaggerate any existing weakness e.g. back strain, kidney damage, emotional stress. The supervision of pregnancy is collectively known as ante-natal care.

Ante-natal care as we know it came about due to the very large numbers of women who died in childbirth, or shortly afterwards, and children who died during the first 2 years of life. With the growth of ante-natal services, greater public awareness of its necessity and improvement in the health of women generally, vital statistics (from the Office of Population Censuses and Surveys) show the sharp decrease in maternal and infant mortality rates.

The aims of ante-natal care are as follows:

a) to maintain or improve the health of the mother
b) to deliver her at term of a healthy living infant
c) to detect any abnormality and treat it where possible
d) to educate the mother for labour and **lactation**
e) to educate the parents in child development and parenthood in order to assist the establishment of satisfactory physical and mental relationships.

It is hoped to achieve these aims by means of regular medical examination, practice for labour and post-natal recovery, advice on personal hygiene, parentcraft classes, provision of supplementary dietary requirements and government financial help.

CONCEPTION
During intercourse mature sperms are deposited by the penis at the neck of the womb. They are contained in a fluid known as semen. A teaspoonful (5 ml) of semen has been estimated to

contain 200,000,000 sperms. This excess is nature's means of providing for continuation of the human race. She leaves nothing to chance.

In normal circumstances, the woman's ovaries, working alternately, release one ripe egg in every menstrual cycle (about 28 days). This egg is passed into the **oviduct** (Fallopian tube) and starts its journey to the womb. It can only live for 2–3 days unless fertilisation takes place i.e. a mature sperm enters the egg and it begins to develop.

The sperms are released as near to the ripe egg (ovum) in the woman's body as is possible. Conditions at the neck of the womb are right for their survival and it is fair to assume that with odds of 200,000,000 sperms to 1 ovum, fertilisation will take place if a ripe ovum is accessible.

However, the journey from the neck of the womb (cervix) to the oviduct has been estimated as the equivalent of a human being swimming 6 miles, so it is not surprising that some sperms die on the way, and that some lose their way and may stray into the oviduct which does not contain an egg.

Intercourse will, of course, in a satisfactory relationship, take place at intervals throughout the menstrual cycle. In order to conceive, intercourse must take place at that stage in the cycle when the ripe ovum has been released and is travelling towards the womb. This is easily calculated in the knowledge of a woman's menstrual pattern. A doctor, midwife or health visitor will advise prospective parents regarding this matter.

Assuming that intercourse occurs around the ovulation period, the first sperm to reach the egg penetrates the outer 'shell'. Immediately, that 'shell' becomes tough and resists the attempts at penetration by other sperms. From that moment the woman is pregnant. Already, due to chromosome activity, some characteristics are decided and the child is developing.

The fertilised ovum completes its journey to the womb, the lining of which has been preparing to receive and nurture the developing **embryo**. Growth and development result from the division and multiplication of cells to form the embryo which implants itself in the lining of the womb.

The commonest first sign of pregnancy is cessation of the menstrual flow (period). In a healthy woman, having regular intercourse and an otherwise regular menstrual pattern, this would be regarded as a cardinal sign. However, it is not uncommon for a woman to 'miss' a second period before consulting her doctor for a diagnosis of pregnancy, but increasingly women will request a pregnancy test before this, usually at around the 6th week.

In any event, it is essential that a doctor is consulted as early in the pregnancy as is practical, in order that recordings of blood tests, urine tests, weight, blood pressure and general health may be made. These early results provide a base line with which later recordings may be compared. It is important for those supervising the pregnancy to know the blood type and Rhesus factor, the normal blood pressure, the rate of weight gain and any health defect e.g. kidney weakness or venereal disease in order that prompt treatment may be given.

A knowledge of the woman's normal menstrual pattern and date of the 1st day of the last normal period will enable her doctor or midwife to estimate the expected date of delivery. This is a piece of information which will affect subsequent preparation for the child.

One decision which must be taken almost immediately, following confirmation of pregnancy, is where the baby will be delivered. The possibilities are home confinement conducted by a domiciliary midwife or family doctor, hospital delivery, or in a private nursing home. The choice will be made in the light of the mother's health and preference, financial state, home circumstances and the availability of hospital and nursing home beds. Another factor which may influence this decision is whether or not the parents wish the father to be present during the delivery. This is an important factor, since it relates to parents' emotions and one about which they may hold strong views. Increasingly, the medical profession is encouraging the father to attend, because many mothers derive support from his presence and the father derives great satisfaction from assisting his partner in their joint emotional experience.

Whilst all these arrangements are being made, the embryo is passing through one of the most vital periods of its development. We left the embryo embedded in the wall of the uterus, now let us centre attention on some of the remarkable changes taking place.

A TIMETABLE OF FOETAL DEVELOPMENT

During the first 3 weeks, the whole structure including the sac is known as the ovum. The ovum becomes implanted in the wall of the uterus which has been preparing to receive and nurture it. The cell mass of the ovum puts out roots which secure it to the uterine wall and provide the means by which the growing ovum will receive nutritious substances.

Already the cells have begun to differentiate, forming the **mesoderm** from which the circulatory, skeletal and muscular systems will develop; the **endoderm** from which the digestive and some glandular systems grow, and the **ectoderm** from which the sense organs and nervous system will develop.

From the 3rd to 8th week the term *embryo* is used. The structure now is remarkably sophisticated. Still less than 1 cm, the embryo is curved like a bean with the rudiments of arms and legs. Centres of ossification (see p. 40) are apparent in some cases and hands and feet are recognisable. The head already has the greatest proportions, shows evidence of features and encloses the brain. The digestive tract, liver and kidneys are budding and the heart tube is pumping steadily.

It is in these early weeks that the embryo is at greatest risk to the effects of adverse environmental factors.

From the 9th week of pregnancy the term *foetus* is used. During the early foetal period the limbs become well formed with marked acceleration of growth in the upper part of the body. Sex organs begin to form and sexual differentiation occurs. Buds for all 20 deciduous teeth are laid down. The digestive system, liver and kidneys show a degree of activity.

In the second half of the foetal stage, greater reflex activity is seen as muscular and neural maturation continue. This can be felt by the mother (**quickening**). The foetal heart can be heard using a foetal stethoscope, or a trace obtained on an **oscilloscope**. The skin structures begin to attain their final form and hair and nails appear. Due to the lack of **subcutaneous** fat the foetus is lean and wrinkled. The eyelids, which have been fused since early on in pregnancy, open. Eyelashes and eyebrows develop. The baby's body is covered in a waxy 'complexion cream' known as vernix caseosa.

At the 28th week the foetus is said to be 'viable'. This means that if he is delivered now, technically he is capable of living a

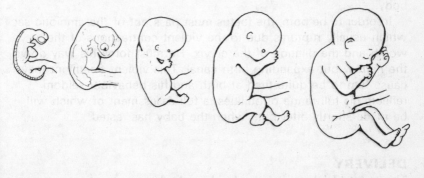

| 32 days | 40 days | 8 weeks | 16 weeks | 20 weeks |

Fig 2.1

Fig 2.2

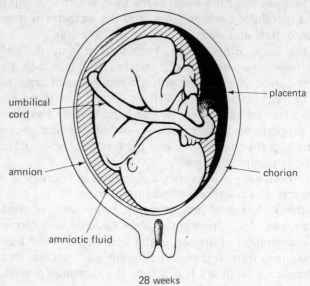

umbilical cord

placenta

amnion

chorion

amniotic fluid

28 weeks

separate existence from his mother. However, he is still very immature in all areas of development and will need meticulous care if life is to be sustained. A very small number of these exceedingly immature babies survive.

During the last 12 weeks finishing touches are being put on the various organs and functions. Fat is formed, smoothing out the wrinkled skin and giving more rounded contours. The digestive organs expel waste products and **meconium** is formed.

Eventually he should settle into the position in which he will be born. Activity decreases as the foetus becomes more restrained by the lack of space in the womb. He will still kick and thrust out his arms in jerky movements but is less likely to turn his whole body.

In order to be born, the foetus must pass out of the amniotic sac which usually ruptures due to the violent contractions of the womb and the dilation of the cervix. He must force his way down the narrow but expanding birth canal. This violent treatment may cause him to be quite tired at birth and his behaviour seldom reflects his full range of abilities, a full assessment of which will be made shortly after birth when the baby has rested.

DELIVERY

The onset of labour is brought about by hormone action in the woman's body. Early on she will experience a tightening in her abdomen caused by the womb contracting to expel the foetus.

She may also notice that a blood streaked plug of mucus comes away from the vagina – we say 'she has a show' – or the sac of fluid in which the baby has grown bursts and **amniotic fluid** escapes. These two latter signs are an indication that the cervix has started to dilate.

'Labour' is aptly named because it is a period of hard work. The woman uses her knowledge gained from her ante-natal preparation to aid the process of expulsion.

Labour is divided into three stages: the first ends with full dilation of the neck of the womb; the second is marked by the birth of the child; and the third completes the sequence with expulsion of the placenta and membranes. These, having performed their respective functions, are now waste products, and after a brief period of rest following the birth, the womb begins to contract again to rid itself of these waste products.

The close physical bond between mother and child is broken, but the emotional bond is just beginning. This can be enhanced by breast feeding. The mother's body protects her developing child, she summons her physical and psychological strengths to deliver him safely and with breast feeding she can fulfil the third function for which she is designed.

Motherhood is a role which needs to be learned. The early days

Fig 2.3   '... the emotional bond is just beginning.'

of establishing a relationship with her child is a deeply emotional experience during which she will need support, guidance, physical help and understanding, to adjust satisfactorily. A new responsibility is accepted and one which no mother can underestimate. Upon her will depend the survival and healthy development of her child.

THE FULL TERM INFANT (see Table 1)

Soon after delivery, the paediatrician will examine the baby to determine that he has reached the stage of maturity that is expected of a full term infant and to detect any abnormality. This early examination reassures the mother and allows early recordings to be made which serve as a basis for future observation of the child. Should any abnormality be found, early treatment can be effected.

General appearance

The skin of a newborn baby is pink, with the possible exception of the hands and feet which may appear a little blue due to diminished blood circulation in the extremities. This is temporary, and does not usually indicate any heart defect. He should be chubby, due to an adequate covering of subcutaneous fat. His head is very large in comparison with the rest of his body. His overall proportions are rather fish-like: largest at the upper part of the body and becoming smaller towards the legs. The umbilicus is well below the mid-line. A large number of babies have minimal peeling of the skin on the hands and feet. Unless the skin is very dry and there is peeling and cracking of the skin on the torso, this flakiness does not indicate postmaturity.

The skull circumference in a baby of average weight (3.4 kg) should measure 343 mm. The posterior fontanelle is just palpable and the anterior fontanelle is felt as a depression of approximately 2.5–4 cm. A degree of overriding of the skull bones occurs during birth, due to the pressure of the birth canal. This occurs at the **sutures** and is known as **moulding**.

Careful examination of the eyes is made to exclude the possibility of infection which may have been contacted during birth and any sign of injury. Any abnormality of the mouth is usually seen immediately; however, the roof of the mouth must be examined to exclude a **cleft palate**.

The distended abdomen should be seen to rise and fall with respiration. At this early stage, the clamped cord will still be soft and pliable. The safety of the clamp is checked now and frequently over the next 24 hours to ensure that no bleeding takes place.

The fingers and toes are counted and any extra digits or webbing noted and treated. The skin folds will harbour excess vernix and this should be removed before it hardens and causes soreness. The spine and buttocks must be examined for presence of a **sinus**. The **patency** of the anus must be checked.

Observation of the **genitalia** is made to check the satisfactory structure of the organs and note that there is no obstruction to the flow of urine. The baby girl may show protrusion of the labia minora. These folds of skin will soon become protected as fatty tissue fills out the labia majora. The baby boy's scrotum is gently palpated to locate the testes which have developed in the abdomen and should have tracked down to lie outside the body in the scrotum. Occasionally, the journey becomes arrested and if one or both testes are not in the scrotum, the child must be observed to ensure that they do come down during childhood. A permanent state of undescended testes necessitates surgical correction. The foreskin, covering the tip of the penis, must be relaxed sufficiently to allow the passage of urine. At this stage, the foreskin is attached to the tip of the penis and will not separate to allow full retraction until the child is around 3 years old, or older. The practice of pushing back the foreskin in the bath is not only undesirable, it is positively harmful since exposure of the urethra can give entry to infection, and retraction may tear the foreskin and cause scar tissue to form. Circumcision may be recommended but only for medical reasons. However, it is necessary to respect the religious custom of circumcision in some faiths.

Flexion, abduction and external rotation of the hips is performed to ensure complete mobility and exclude the condition of congenital dislocation of the hip joint.

Posture and movement
Placed on his back, the newborn adopts an asymmetrical posture. He extends one arm and appears to focus upon it. The adoption of this posture can be seen in response to the head being turned. The child will extend the arm on that side. This is known as the tonic neck reflex. His hands are gently closed most of the time. His limbs perform random movements. Pulled to a sitting position, the head will lag behind. If we support him in ventral suspension, the head will fall forward. This head lag is due to its excessive weight and immature muscle tone.

Reflexes
The healthy newborn displays a most interesting collection of reflexes. The presence of these reflexes is an indication of the integrity of the nervous system and a predictor of future nervous maturity.

Table I   Comparison of the average full term baby at birth and the premature baby

	Average full term baby	Premature baby
Maturity	40 weeks	28–40 weeks
Weight	3,400 grammes	less than 2,500 grammes
Length	45–51 cm	depends upon maturity
Proportions (descending order)	head, shoulders, chest and abdomen, hips (umbilicus two-thirds down body)	same order – more exaggerated
Head	circumference – 343 mm a) anterior and posterior **fontanelles** b) sutures c) moulding	circumference – according to maturity fontanelles larger and sutures wider than for full term infant
General appearance	chubby – subcutaneous fat colour – good no body or facial hair – vernix nails umbilical cord	wrinkled – little fat colour – poor lanugo hair – vernix ++ nails – immature may be jaundiced worried expression
Body temperature	38°C – maintains even body temperature	often subnormal
Defaecation	1 meconium 2 **changing stool** 3 infant stool	same, but changing stool period may last longer
Urination	passes urine soon after birth	often poor kidney function (immature kidneys)

indicate some kidney function in the uterus. In the womb, most of the baby's excretion was conducted by the mother via the placenta and her excretion mechanisms.

At birth, the kidneys become the prime organ of excretion for the baby and are required to be active almost immediately. It is necessary to observe the period of time between delivery and the passing of urine by the child, otherwise some obstruction in the urinary tract may go unnoticed. However, it may be 24–48 hours before the first urination is noticed and this time lapse should give no anxiety providing that the child appears healthy and the bladder is not distended.

Much will depend on the amounts of fluid taken at this time, and the frequency of urination will rise proportionately to the fluid intake. However, the child should excrete some of the excess fluid which has accumulated in the tissues prior to delivery. Again, this tissue fluid is a store to make up for the time lapse between the sudden break from the mother at delivery until the fluid intake rises to a satisfactory and safe level to maintain life.

It seems relevant to discuss the weight pattern at this stage. This pattern is greatly influenced by the rate of establishment of feeding, but there is always a weight loss in the first few days caused by the removal of excess fluid and the relatively low food intake. As soon as lactation starts or artificial milk feeding is established, the weight will steadily rise and the child will regain his birth weight within the first 8–10 days of life. From then on, he should gain approximately 150–180 gm per week in the first 3 months.

Hormone imbalance

A small, hard swelling around the nipples of both boys and girls and the extrusion of a milky fluid is not uncommon. This is due to a temporary hormone imbalance. It need cause no anxiety and the mother should be reassured that it will resolve spontaneously. Treatment is only required if there are signs of inflammation.

For a similar reason, we occasionally find baby girls having a small vaginal haemorrhage similar to menstruation. This should be noted and observed, but no treatment is indicated. The flow is small in amount and will cease spontaneously.

The heart

The heart is composed of very specialised muscle tissue known as cardiac muscle. Nowhere in the body do we find muscle like it. It is unique in that, in health, it beats rhythmically and continuously from the early months of foetal life until it ceases at death. This pattern is only altered by fear, anxiety, exercise,

Fig 2.4   normal circulation through the heart

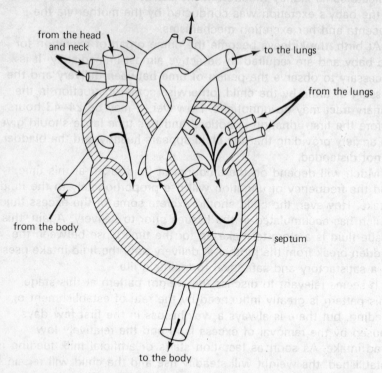

from the head
and neck

to the lungs

from the lungs

from the body

septum

to the body

excitement, when its rate increases, or by rest and sleep, when
the rate slows. The heart is located in the chest between
the lungs.

The foetal heart can be heard clearly using a foetal stethoscope
from the 20th week of pregnancy. At this time, its rate is rapid
and can be described as fluttering. During infancy and childhood
the rate slows from the normal 120–140 beats per minute of the
newborn baby to the average 72–80 beats per minute of the adult.

The function of the heart is to pump blood round the body,
distributing nutrition and oxygen to all the tissues. At the same
time, waste products are collected from the tissues and taken to
the various organs of excretion e.g. the lungs, the skin, the
kidneys. Hormones are also transported by blood.

Blood travels through two kinds of tubes: the arteries which
carry blood away from the heart; and veins which convey blood
back to the heart. Connecting these two types of vessels is a fine
network of capillaries.

As well as the general circulation, there is a small circuit, the
pulmonary circuit. These vessels are concerned with conveying
blood to the lungs, where waste substances are extracted and

breathed out and oxygen is collected for general distribution. The foetal circulation is specially arranged to take account of the fact that the lungs are not functioning for respiration and only require sufficient blood supply to grow and develop.

In the adult, the two halves of the heart are separated by a wall known as the septum (see Figure 2.4). This division runs longitudinally down the heart, separating oxygenated blood from blood that has been deoxygenated. In the foetus, a valve exists (1) between the right and left sides of the heart to permit some of the blood to bypass the lungs. An additional bypass is the ductus arteriosus (2), a small tube which directs blood from the pulmonary artery to the aorta (see Figure 2.5). With the first inspiration, the lungs inflate and the resulting suction causes the flap valve in the septum to close and the walls of the ductus arteriosus to collapse, obliterating the connection between pulmonary artery and aorta. From now on the left and right sides of the heart will be quite separate and the ductus arteriosus will no longer be patent.

Occasionally, these two closing mechanisms fail and congenital heart defects exist.

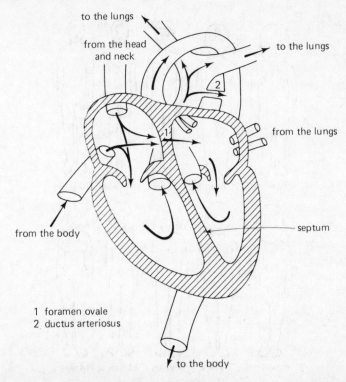

1 foramen ovale
2 ductus arteriosus

Fig 2.5   circulation through the foetal heart

3
Mobility

BODY PROPORTIONS

At birth, the head forms one quarter of the child's total length. The head circumference is greater than the chest circumference. The baby appears to have no neck. The arms are longer than the legs. The umbilicus is well below the mid-line of his total length. The greatest degree of development so far has taken place in the head and upper part of the body.

This 'top-heavy' development militates against good balance and must be modified before he can sit, stand and walk. In children with gross proportional abnormality e.g. hydrocephalus or obesity

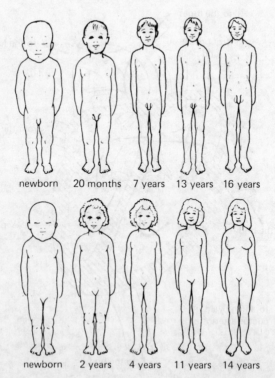

| newborn | 20 months | 7 years | 13 years | 16 years |

| newborn | 2 years | 4 years | 11 years | 14 years |

Fig 3.1   changing proportions

walking is greatly delayed.

The superior intellect of the human being dictated functions which made an upright posture necessary. In doing so, the full weight of the body was thrown on to the legs, which subsequently developed sufficient strength to bear the strain. Hence, by full maturity, the legs have become the largest and strongest parts of the body.

The head

Growth of the head slows after birth. Elizabeth Hurlock* has estimated that the head of a man 1.8 m tall would measure approximately 40 cm in length instead of the average 20–22 cm, if it were to continue its growth at the pre-natal rate.

Development of the head is affected by growth of the structures within it e.g. the eyes, the teeth, the nose and the sinuses, the brain. Simultaneously, the baby chubbiness goes away, the face grows downwards and forwards resulting in a more angular outline.

Neck and trunk

Compounding this 'top-heavy' distribution of weight is the gross development of the upper trunk. The desired change in proportions comes about by lengthening of the neck, trunk and legs.

The child approaching walking ability does so not only because his nervous system is maturing and he has received proper encouragement and care, but also because his trunk and legs have lengthened to provide a balance of weight in the lower half of his body and toppling is less likely. At this stage, the umbilicus appears nearer to the mid-line of the total body length.

The chest

At birth, the chest is rounded due to the high shoulders and horizontal lie of the ribs. These proportions are related to the larger abdomen containing the enlarged liver which takes up space later filled by the expanding right lung. The newborn, because of this horizontal lie of the ribs, depends almost entirely on the movements of the diaphragm to enlarge the chest cavity and bring about satisfactory respiration (diaphragmatic breathing). Between the 3rd and 10th years of life the ribs acquire an oblique lie, resulting in a broadening and flattening of the chest. The shoulders drop and the neck appears to lengthen. The lungs increase in size as the rib cage increases and the chest gradually takes on larger proportions than the abdomen.

* *Child Development*, by Elizabeth Hurlock. McGraw Hill, 1973.

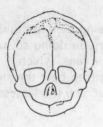

Growth of the face is affected by development of the structures inside.

The face grows downwards and forwards.

skull at birth

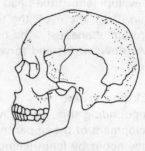

skull of an adult

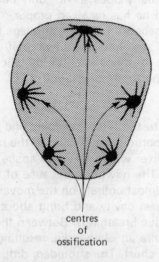

centres
of
ossification

In the foetus, the brain is covered by a sheet of membrane.

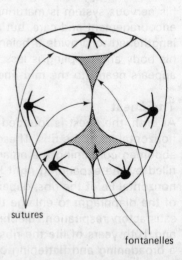

sutures

fontanelles

The skull at birth has this degree of ossification. The remaining membrane areas are known as fontanelles.

Fig 3.2   development of the skull

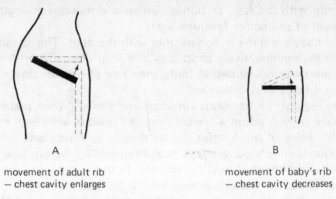

A	B
movement of adult rib — chest cavity enlarges	movement of baby's rib — chest cavity decreases

Fig 3.3   development of the chest

Due to the slow rate of ossification, the chest is very mobile in these developing years. Our care involves provision of freedom to allow the chest to expand fully, fresh air and exercise which will encourage healthy lung function. It is sensible in the early months of life to pay due attention to the humidity level of the atmosphere surrounding the child, in order that the mucus membranes maintain a healthy, moist condition.

During the relatively inactive weeks of a baby's early life, we should put him to sleep on alternate sides to ensure equal lung expansion. The effects of poor chest development include chest deformity and poor lung expansion which may lead to infection. Proper development of the chest is vital for good posture and the satisfactory formation of the vertebral column.

One of the most influential factors in the change of body outline is hormone activity. In childhood, the boy and girl are completely similar in outline. As puberty approaches, the sex hormones cause the typical masculine and feminine outlines to begin their development. The young man ultimately takes on a triangular body shape, broad at the shoulders, narrow at the waist and hips. The young woman takes on softer, more rounded contours suited to the function of childbearing.

Arms and legs
The upper and lower limbs are constructed in very similar fashion. The main difference is that, due to the evolutionary changes which have resulted in our upright posture leaving hands and arms free from involvement in mobility, the bones of the hands are lighter in weight and have developed fine skill rather than strength.

Like the feet, the hands at birth are chubby and the terminal bones in the fingers are present as tiny seeds of cartilage. In common with the feet, as bones harden and muscles strengthen, the layer of protective fat goes away.

The baby's outline is comparable with the apes. This is largely due to his comparatively short legs and long arms. Because the arms are more developed at birth, their rate of growth slows during infancy and childhood.

The legs of the newborn are short and flexed. When placed on his back he will adopt a typical frog-like posture with legs everted and the soles of the feet facing. As their length increases throughout childhood, the legs straighten and by the 6th year of life the legs and knees should be straight. In the upright posture, thighs, knees, calves and ankles should be touching.

During this straightening process posture defects occur. The child 1 year old has only begun to straighten his legs and we commonly see a degree of bow-leggedness at this stage. Later, around 4 years, it is not unusual to see a slight knock knee. These are normal at the stages of development described, but should not persist.

The tiny hands and feet must increase in size as well as muscular development. Fine manipulation gradually becomes possible as the fingers lengthen, the terminal bones continue to ossify and the baby fat disperses. Comparable development of the toes is essential for the balance required for walking.

A knowledge of this changing pattern is essential to our care of young children since proportions affect the child's physical function and personality.

As we have observed, growth is continuous, but is subjected to spurts in rate. In early childhood, when the proportions are

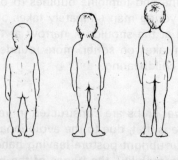

18 months   3 years   6 years
(bow legs) (knock knees) (legs straight)

Fig 3.4   normal posture

changing most rapidly, there may be temporary loss of body control. This, in part, gives rise to some of the frustrations seen in the child in his 2nd and 3rd years of life. His body does not behave as he would wish. Tolerance, patience and often humour are our best tools for dealing with this situation, since anger and disapproval will only increase the frustration.

Proportions affect appearance. A pleasing appearance is important for self confidence. The chubby, cuddly child invariably appeals to adults. Attractive children tend to receive more attention. The child passing through the 'ugly duckling' stage senses he is unattractive and may withdraw into himself or behave in an anti-social, attention-seeking way. This stage coincides with secondary dentition and a lengthening of the face. He has gaps in his teeth, his mouth seems too large for his face and he may experience difficulty in controlling the excess saliva which collects in his mouth. The spindly arms and legs at this time make the feet and hands seem too big.

The cuddly child often creates the impression that he is less mature than he is. The lean 'leggy' child may look more mature. An awareness of this may prevent underestimation of the one and over expectancy of the other.

BONE DEVELOPMENT

Movement comes about due to muscles pulling on bones under control of the brain and nervous system. The brain is the command centre which communicates with other parts of the body by means of a network of nerves. This is a two-way method of communication. The eyes, ears, nose, taste organs and skin receive and transmit information to the brain. If those messages demand movement, signals are returned to specific muscles in order to bring about the desired action.

The body framework is supplied by the skeleton, a collection of bones, each designed to perform a particular function whilst collectively providing support (e.g. the neck supports the head) and protection (e.g. the rib cage protects the lungs, heart and other vital structures situated within).

The skeleton performs two other less obvious but equally vital functions. Blood cells are manufactured in bone and calcium, and other minerals are stored here to be called upon if required.

Bone begins its development early in foetal life. X-ray pictures have clearly shown the outlines of tiny bones as early as the 12th week of pregnancy. Bone develops in 3 ways:

1 from cartilage (e.g. the bones of the limbs, which are rods of bone) – *long bones*

2 from membrane (e.g. the skull bones, which are plates of bone) — *flat bones* (see Figure 3.2)

3 from tiny seeds within tendons (e.g. the knee cap, the small bones of the ankle and wrist — all of which are irregular 'cubes' of bone) — ***sesamoid bones***

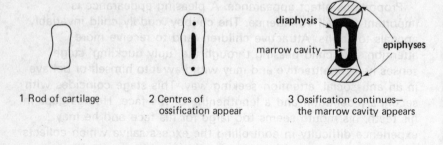

1 Rod of cartilage   2 Centres of ossification appear   3 Ossification continues—the marrow cavity appears

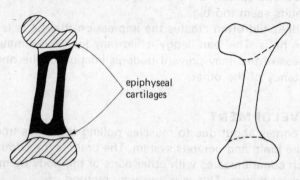

4 Growth now takes place at the epiphyseal cartilages   5 Ossification of the epiphyseal cartilages causes fusion of the epiphyses and diaphysis

Fig 3.5   development of a long bone

Through a delicate and complicated process requiring absorption of calcium, vitamin D, phosphorus and other minerals, these soft structures harden and take on the substance of bone. These minerals give the developing bone its strength and rigidity. This process is called ossification. It is a gradual process, commenced in the uterus and completed by 21 years of age.

Bone growth takes place at the bone ends of long bones and the edges of flat bones. In young children the areas of soft material allow large spaces between the bones and joints, which accounts for the flexibility of children's limbs and the easy postures they adopt.

Due to the elasticity of young children's bones, they decrease in stature during the day and regain their height following a night's

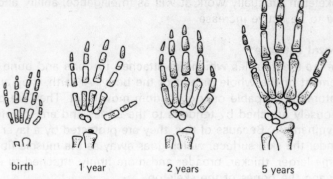

birth   1 year   2 years   5 years

Fig 3.6   skeletal development of the hand and wrist

rest. This may be the origin of the saying that children grow in bed. We have measured a difference of up to 2 cm in the height of a 4 year old at the end of the day compared with a height measurement the following morning. Because of this flexibility, young bones are subject to pressure and muscle pull which can result in dislocation and deformity.

Our care, then, requires a knowledge of these facts in order that we pick up and carry children without causing strain on their joints; that we provide cots, prams, furniture, clothing and shoes that will allow freedom for normal development to take place. We must avoid prolonged periods in one posture e.g. standing. Also, we must ensure a diet containing adequate amounts of minerals, particularly calcium, phosphorus and vitamin D. Periods of the day must be programmed for exercise, balanced by adequate periods of rest. We must provide incentives for movement, the most suitable play material and opportunities to suit the stage of development in safe surroundings. Protection against infection is of vital importance, since growing bone has a very rich blood supply and may readily receive any invading infecting organism.

MUSCULAR DEVELOPMENT

Various types of muscle exist in the body, the structure of each differing from the others according to the function performed. The newborn baby has all the muscles present in his body that he will ever need. Maturity brings increase in size and efficiency, which is measured in terms of strength. Muscles in good condition are said to have 'tone'; neglected muscles are said to be 'flaccid'.

A baby's early movements are largely reflex i.e. they are not performed under conscious control. Some muscle activity never does come under conscious control, but the muscles attached to the skeleton gradually work at will as intelligence, ability and the desire to be active increase.

Skeletal muscle

These are the muscles which are attached to bone and bring about movement of the whole or part of the body. At birth, they are immature and capable only of random movement. They are puny and loosely attached by tendons to the bones and are therefore very vulnerable. Because of this, they are protected by a layer of fat under the skin surface, which goes away as the muscle fibres become larger, thicker, broader and more firmly attached to each other and the bones of the skeleton.

The healthy child has a strong desire to be active and is constantly 'on the go'. If he is restrained, he becomes restless and fidgets. Children tire easily, but with a short period of rest will completely recover and be ready to go again, almost before the adult has caught his breath. Despite this quick recovery, it is important that the supervising adult recognises the early signs of fatigue and provides quiet times to compensate and allow young muscles to recharge themselves. This cycle of events goes on throughout the day, complete recuperation being obtained after satisfactory sleep.

Children in groups need a well organised but flexible programme of activities, balancing large physical activity with more restful ones e.g. table top toys, storytelling, music and singing, television. As well as organised activities, it is also necessary to cater for the individual child who wishes to withdraw from the group at will e.g. to a cosy chair, to a book corner or to the house corner which contains a child-sized bed.

Skeletal muscles rely upon good diet and exercise balanced by rest for their satisfactory condition. In common with other body structures, muscles improve with use. It is not surprising then that, following illness, muscle tone is poor and an adequate convalescence with gradual increase in mobility is necessary to ensure complete recovery. Where there is prolonged poor diet and lack of exercise, muscle wasting occurs. The muscles become flaccid and careful management is necessary to correct this condition.

Skeletal muscles are affected greatly by hereditary characteristics, particularly racial features. The negro babies seem more muscular at birth and retain this superiority for several years. Asian children appear more puny, but muscle size bears little relation to efficiency and strength. Other factors affecting this area of development include diet, exercise balanced by rest, opportunity, space, freedom. Large motor skills only develop when the child has access to climbing apparatus, large bricks/blocks, balls, tricycles and later bicycles. The ideal play area will include safe, fixed structures, such as are found in an adventure playground. It is also possible and desirable to make use of discarded materials such as rubber tyres, sewer pipes, packing cases, tree trunks etc. Any town or country area has sources of materials which the imaginative and observant adult can exploit.

THE VERTEBRAL COLUMN AND POSTURE

The vertebral column (spine) is a flexible rod, formed from small, cube-like bones stacked one upon another and separated by pads of cartilage. These act as shock absorbers and make the spine flexible. This flexibility gives strength to the spine and is vital if we are to have a full range of movement.

In childhood, as we have seen, the process of ossification is only partially complete and if we were to X-ray the spine of a young baby we would see very large areas of cartilage between the bones. Due to the confines of the womb, the child is moulded. This is most noticeable in the spine which forms a long curve, concave arterially.

As time goes by, and due to an increase in the child's activities, later curves develop. The small muscles attached to the spine are strengthening too and it is largely due to muscle pull that the curves form. These curves are essential to our upright posture and balance since it is their presence which gives the spine its strength and mobility.

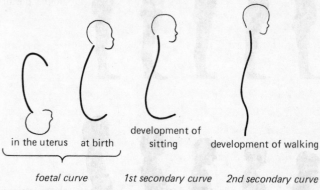

| | | development of | |
| in the uterus | at birth | sitting | development of walking |

foetal curve   *1st secondary curve*   *2nd secondary curve*

Fig 3.7   spinal curve

The new baby spends the first few days of his life stretching and moving without the confines of the strong muscular organ which previously contained him. More and more he likes to stretch his legs and arms and lie straight when awake, but when sleeping he often reverts to his foetal position — the spine curved, knees and

47

hips flexed, arms across his chest. This is a 'comfort posture'. A posture that makes him feel secure and one to which children and adults revert in times of stress or fatigue. If we take his hands and pull him to a sitting position, his head will lag behind as we raise him and then flop forward or to one side. In this position, we see clearly demonstrated the primary or foetal curve in the spine. Before long, within 4–6 weeks, he will be able to turn his head freely from side to side. Within a few weeks more he will confidently hold his head in the mid-line when supported in the sitting position (3–4 months). This helps the formation of the neck curve.

The development of an upright posture proceeds downwards in this way conforming to one of our basic principles of development. As sitting ability improves, and later crawling and walking occur, the later curves will form. Until the proportions change and permit a more even distribution of weight, some of the spinal curves will be exaggerated and the child may take compensatory measures e.g. placing his feet wide apart.

The bones of his pelvis are, at this stage, separated by pads of cartilage. His lower limbs have chased the development of his arms and overtaken, but this burst of development in the lower

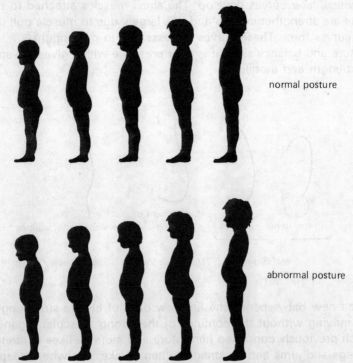

normal posture

abnormal posture

Fig 3.8

limbs plus the mobility of the pelvis gives rise to a bow-legged posture around 12–18 months. This is a normal posture at this time and should right itself with continued good diet, exercise, rest etc. Particularly important is freedom; from restricting clothing e.g. bulky napkins, tight shoes and socks; from restricting bed clothes. As the legs become firmer and straighter, we may find a temporary knock knee, at around 3–4 years. Again, this is not a cause for worry, since it should right itself by the time the child is 6 years old.

FEET

The new baby's feet are chubby and dimpled. The toes appear short and the heel very small. If we took a self-inking pad and made a foot print, we would see that the foot is almost triangular in shape — broad at the toes and narrow at the heel. This is due to several factors. The bones of the foot develop as for all long bones and at birth are very pliable. The toe bones are the last to ossify and at birth the terminal toe bone is merely a seed of cartilage at the beginning of its development. The ankle bones develop like sesamoid bones and many have just begun their development at birth (proximodistal development). These pliable bones, with large spaces between them, leave the foot very vulnerable. Nature compensates for this by protecting these immature little bones with a large pad of fat.

As the hardening of these bones progresses, the muscles which attach to them become stronger, the child becomes more active and the four arches of the foot develop. This takes place due to muscle pulling on pliable bones and bending them to form curves which give the foot its strength and flexibility and allow the child to develop agility, balance and speed. Simultaneously, the protective pad of fat is absorbed.

Excluding diet, the most important factor which contributes to this healthy development is exercise with freedom. Throughout infancy, childhood and into adult life, we should set aside a period of the day when the feet are free of shoes and socks or tights. Do we ever see the degrees of deformity of the hands that we see in the feet? If we permitted the freedom for our feet that we give our hands many adults would lead more active and less painful lives.

Shoes are only necessary as a means of protection against roads, pavements and harmful things which could damage the feet. With this in mind, it becomes evident that the child only needs shoes when he becomes sufficiently skilled at walking to go for short walks outside. We must ensure ease of movement in bed clothes and socks, prams, cots etc, which allow the child to stretch his length without hindrance and provide firm, safe surfaces for exercise.

Occasionally, when defects occur, shoes take on a different role. They become supportive. Corrective shoes may be prescribed in the following common postural defects, seen in children:

pronation — internal rotation of foot due to weak muscles on the inner border; this condition is often accompanied by varying degrees of bow legs

toes pointing out — due to weak ankle muscles and often accompanied by a degree of knock knee

flat foot — due to poor development of arches.

In each of these cases, supportive shoes will prevent fatigue but correction is more swiftly aided by barefoot activities e.g. toe wiggling, ankle rotation, walking on toes, picking up objects with toes, walking in a straight line. In childhood it is possible to make these exercises fun times. They can be incorporated into musical and percussion times. Children could try exploring paint, clay, water and sand with toes, as well as hands. Older children should do all gymnastics and movement sessions in bare feet, providing that the floor surface is safe.

DEVELOPMENT OF AN UPRIGHT POSTURE AND WALKING

Due to the child's inherent desire to be active and with developing co-ordination of bones and muscles, our helpless, relatively immobile baby becomes an independent mobile infant. This great achievement is gradual, continuous and predictable, with progress culminating in confident walking at between 1 year and 18 months. The progress is predictable in that all babies must sit before they can crawl and stand before they walk. It can be said that walking development begins in the uterus with unco-ordinated foetal movements. At birth, the child has a well developed walking and kicking reflex; both of which, as we have seen, accommodate a temporary need and go away in order that the voluntary action can develop. In common with other areas of development, the pattern of increasing mobility conforms with the head to tail direction of development (cephalocaudal).

Whilst it is important to recognise average ages at which stages of development are reached, it is more important to observe that the child is in fact passing through the stages in sequence and watch for the approach of the next stage in order that we may encourage it and cater for it. Great **anxiety** is experienced where a child does not conform precisely to a timetable of development and, whilst the average is given, it is important to stress that some children will be ahead or behind the average at certain stages, but the end result will prove satisfactory.

At birth, he lies in the position in which we put him. If that position is on his back, he will stretch one arm, turn his head and apparently look towards it, hands closed; the other arm moves in a random fashion. His legs flex and he lies with the soles of his feet facing. There is noticeably more movement in the upper part of the body than in the lower part. Placed on his abdomen, the youngest baby will turn his head to one side, some will attempt to raise the head from the flat surface, only to fall back a few seconds later due to muscle immaturity. The rest of the body adopts a modified foetal position — knees and hips flexed, arms folded beneath him. Provided the surface is firm i.e. no pillow is present, this is a position in which many babies are content and it has the advantage of being completely safe.

Within a month he will attempt to lift his head away from the supporting shoulder, allowing it to 'bob' hazardously from side to side. This experience is necessary for the developing neck muscles to become stronger, but should last a few seconds only before his mother's hand supports his head.

If we raise him to a sitting position, the head still lags behind, but as early as this we notice attempts at self help, indicated by a tightening of the muscles, in the shoulders and arms.

Lifting his very heavy head is easier for the baby when lying on his front. A period during the day in this position will encourage the child to raise his head and so gradually strengthen the muscles in his neck and shoulders. Within a few weeks he will respond to his mother's extended arms by lifting his head, indicating his desire to rise. On being raised to a sitting position the degree of head lag will have decreased and, with support of his trunk, it will be noticed that the head is now controlled in the mid-line. He turns to observe the world around him and will very quickly demand to be raised during his waking hours. The simultaneous development in his arms will cause him to bring his hands into the mid-line and examine them, visually and orally.

Following the principle of downward development, control of the arms and trunk follows, so that he will sit unsupported for a short while. Commonly, the baby will fall forward on extended arms to support himself and, with a shuffling movement of his buttocks and legs, he will adopt a crawling posture. Alternatively, placed on his front he will flex his knees and hips to acquire this position. Some babies shuffle in a sitting position and never

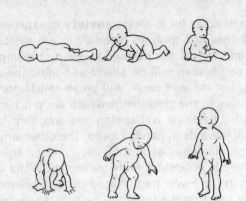

Fig 3.9   development of an upright posture

actually crawl at all. This is unimportant. What matters is that the child adopts some means of becoming mobile, however crude.

Very soon, with the opportunity to practise his new skill, and with encouragement from an interested adult, he will arrive at some means of support by which he can pull himself to a standing position. There is usually much collapsing of the legs until this 'game' brings about a strengthening of the legs and he stands supported for increasing periods.

Due to lack of efficiency, he may frequently revert to shuffling or crawling because he can get where he wants to go more confidently and therefore more quickly. However, it will not be long before he attempts a few sideways steps and begins to cruise around the furniture. Changing direction is a problem though and he will often sit down to change direction until he becomes more controlled and more aware of distance and relative positions of things around him.

Confident, unaided walking is not far away, and the adult can help by assisting him, hands held from behind. It is vital that the adult stands behind him in order that he retains his sense of adventure.

Once independent movement is achieved, the 'world is his oyster'. Running, skipping and hopping naturally follow.

4
Exercise and sleep

Exercise

The young baby acquires all the exercise he needs despite his
immobility. Sucking and crying are forms of very strenuous
exercise. The baby who falls asleep after his feed does so not
merely due to the contentment which comes from a full stomach,
but also due to the tiredness that comes from feeding. We
recognise this in our management of the immature or ill baby,
whom we tube feed in order to protect him from this fatigue.

The crying baby expresses his discontent with his whole body.
The more distressed he becomes, the harder he exercises and the
more tired he will become if he is not comforted.

Later he will show pleasure in this very physical way. He will
clasp his hands together and kick his feet at the presence of his
favourite people, and if one should extend arms to lift him, he will
strain to raise his head and shoulders to assist. Placed in his pram,
he will kick against the bottom. Placed on his front, he will enjoy
raising his head, arms and legs and engage in swimming
movements.

A firm, safe surface will supply all the incentive he needs for
exercise at the crawling stage. A ball or colourful object, not to
say an interested adult, to crawl towards, will increase the pleasure.
Reaching, grasping, crude attempts at feeding himself, are
excellent means of exercising his developing muscles. Exercising in
a baby bouncer may be suitable for short periods when he has
gained control of his head and trunk, but is no substitute for
bouncing on an adult's knee, with all the opportunities for
socialisation which accompany the game. Rough and tumble
games, bath play, pat-a-cake, throwing and retrieving objects
provide most enjoyable forms of exercise.

As mobility and independence increase, the young child will
respond to his curiosity drive and will need close supervision to
protect him from harm. Stairs are great fun to climb, but the adult
must be there to guide the descent.

The pre-schooler will regulate his own exercise and rest periods
to some extent. He will run about and, when tired, flop down

until he recovers. A relatively short walk in the park will tire little legs and feet; a push chair ride at the right moment will avoid a potential conflict situation from arising. A strong adult willing to give a 'piggy-back' at this time is also a great joy.

From about 4 years on, ensuring that a child obtains sufficient suitable exercise needs a degree of thought and management by the adult. Numerous opportunities exist for physical play, whether for a child alone at home or children in groups at nursery school or playgroup. Space, freedom and incentives are the key words, if the child is to establish the lifelong habit of regular exercise, which will be such a good investment for a healthy life.

The adult who does not recognise a child's need to be active will find that the child becomes frustrated, and then lethargic. His appetite may wane and he is less likely to sleep as well as the more fortunate child.

Finally, exercise at any age, taken in the fresh air, is always more beneficial. Rest, and the replenishment of food and oxygen supplies, will quickly revive the small child. Sedentary occupations interspersed with physical activities will benefit the child in two ways: first, his muscles recover their tone; second, concentration

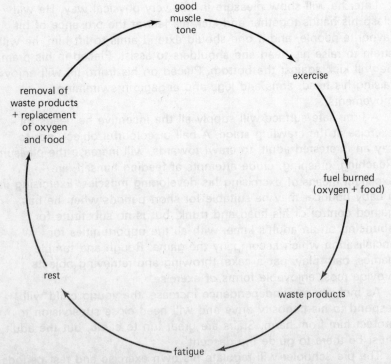

Fig 4.1   physical exercise cycle

Fig 4.2   '... a level of consciousness which blots out external and internal stimuli ...'

changes, from the attention needed for balance, judging distance and making quick responses, to interests of a different nature, which use different senses and require different responses.

Sleep
Sleep is a very special kind of rest. Sleep is a level of unconsciousness which blots out external and internal stimuli. Two types of sleep exist: namely, deep relaxing sleep and rapid eye movement (R.E.M.) or dream sleep. These two occur in cycles during the period of sleep.

We do not fall asleep all at once. It is not a case of consciousness one moment and unconsciousness the next. The body and mind behave rather like the lights of a house when the residents retire for the night. Parts of the body and mind switch off, just as individual lamps in the house are switched off. This can result in muscle twitching, a feeling of falling through the bed or strange thoughts coming into the mind during the settling time. Eventually, all the lights go out and, like the inanimate house, we sleep.

The rapid eye movement (R.E.M.) sleep is the time when the brain sorts out the problems of the day. Some information is committed to memory, whilst irrelevant information is rejected. We need to complete periods of dream sleep in order to awaken mentally refreshed. If we wake within a few minutes of the period of dream sleep, the dream is often remembered. The physical rest that comes during sleep allows the child's bones to regain their length and the muscles to return to a state of good tone.

People who are roused during the R.E.M. period of sleep may be disorientated and find judgement and clear thinking difficult.

Individual needs for sleep vary. Sleep cannot be enforced; it must be encouraged by a sensible daytime programme and a quiet, secure period before bed. The baby quickly develops a sleep pattern which is related to his needs for food. If we respect these needs and behave accordingly, he will pass through a well recognised developmental pattern. Initially, he will take periods of sleep at regular intervals throughout 24 hours. By the end of his 1st year, he will usually adopt a pattern of taking the greatest amount of sleep at night, with one or two naps in the day.

During the 2nd year, many babies adopt a routine of play at bedtime. After being put to bed they get up, walk around the cot, play, burble, fuss and finally fall asleep, usually the wrong way round and with bottom in the air. Perhaps we would expect the late sleeper to awaken late. Unfortunately for his parents, this

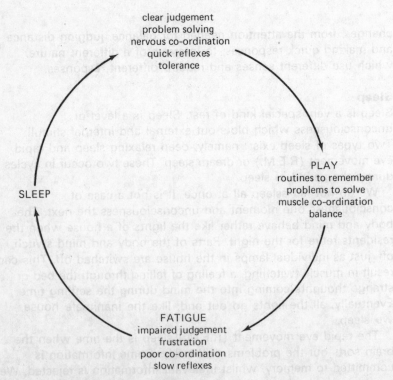

Fig 4.3   mental exercise cycle

child will often wake early too, gurgling with joy at the new day and becoming noisier the longer he is ignored.

As the day becomes more exciting and stimulating, the pre-schooler will find more important things to do than sleep. He will discard the daytime nap and take his greatest amount of sleep at night. However, it is not uncommon to find a small child of this age fast asleep in a heap under a table or in some other secure hidy-hole.

Of course, the young child does not always know what is best for him and, even if he is not ready to sleep, he should be given the opportunity before he becomes so over stimulated that he cannot sleep. Naturally, he will want to assert his independence on occasions and we must be flexible within sensible limits.

Physiology of sleep
During sleep, all the body functions slow down as if to recharge in readiness for the demands of the next day. The heart rate decreases, consequently blood pressure falls and the body temperature drops; the rate and depth of respiration decrease; enzyme production, **peristalsis** and urine production are diminished. If the child is to gain full benefit from sleep, he must be kept warm, free from restriction, and should not take a heavy meal prior to retiring.

5
Vision and manipulation

VISION

The eyes are mounted on a pad of fat in the bony orbits of the skull. This, together with the eyebrows, eyelids and eyelashes, affords the necessary protection for these delicate and precious organs. Each eye has 6 slender muscles which pull, like the reins on a horse, to move the eyes together. Due to their immaturity in babyhood, it is not uncommon to notice the presence of a transient squint, particularly when the baby is ill or tired.

The iris is a muscle which controls the size of the pupil and consequently controls the amount of light entering the eye. It will be noticed that, as the eyes turn towards strong light, the pupils contract, and in poor light or when the eyes are tired, the pupils dilate to allow access to as much light as possible.

In childhood the eyeball is short from front to back, which accounts for the normal longsightedness. With development, this is corrected, but during the maturing process it is necessary to allow for this discrepancy of vision when choosing visual stimulants for children e.g. play materials, size of implements, pictures, print etc. Careful supervision must be made to ensure that young eyes are not strained by poor light or prolonged attention to fine work.

Binocular vision and **depth perception** do not develop until the child is about 6 years old and, until this time, the child is unable to judge distance accurately and may suffer harm in potentially dangerous situations e.g. crossing roads. The numbers of young children injured each year on our roads are alarming and many may be attributed to this immaturity of vision.

The eyes at birth should be clear and sparkling. A sticky discharge, redness or yellow colouring in the white of the eye are abnormalities. Due to the increase in venereal disease, the practice of instilling antiseptic drops into the eye as a preventive measure has been adopted in many hospitals. Careful inspection is made of the eyes of the newborn, since infection at this time may result in permanent defects in vision and occasionally blindness.

We have an in-built mechanism for cleansing and lubricating the eye. This consists of the tear glands and ducts which

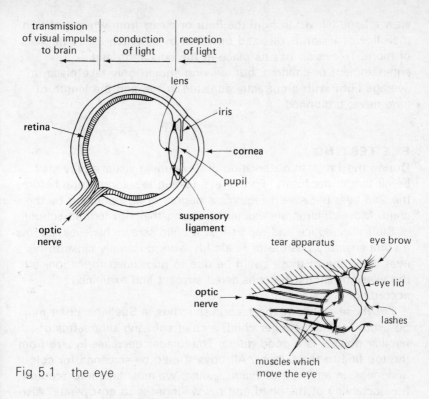

transmission of visual impulse to brain | conduction of light | reception of light

lens

iris

retina

cornea

pupil

suspensory ligament

optic nerve

tear apparatus

eye brow

optic nerve

eye lid

lashes

muscles which move the eye

Fig 5.1   the eye

manufacture mildly antiseptic tears. The tear apparatus is present at birth, but we seldom see tears in the eyes of a baby under 4 weeks, so it follows that the eyes are particularly at risk of infection during this time.

At all times, suitable light should be available for all the activities in which children engage. Natural light is always best, but when artificial light is needed it should be diffused for most general activities and shining over the left or right shoulder for close work. The right handed child will be more comfortable with the source of light behind his left shoulder.

At no time should young eyes be exposed to direct sunlight. Especial care must be taken with the young, immobile baby in this respect and it is wise to remember that a darkened lining on the pram hood is a good investment: a good deal of glare is reflected on to the eyes from a white, shiny surface.

Possibly the greatest hazard to vision is television viewing. Where possible young children should sit at least 1.8 m from an average sized screen, which is placed slightly lower than the line of vision. How often we see young children viewing from the floor and frequently lying on their tummies with their heads propped in cupped hands. How often young children in school view a large television from the floor or chairs from which position their line of vision is directed upwards by as much as 45 degrees or more. Television has its place in the education and entertainment of children, but viewing should only take place in average light with a correctly adjusted image and the length of time never prolonged.

EYE TESTING

During the 1st year, observation of developing visual ability may be all that is necessary. Formal eye testing is seldom done before the 2nd year because it requires a degree of co-operation by the child. Most children are examined during their 1st term in school.

Staff may notice and report that a child screws his eyes, adopts a compensatory posture or holds his work unusually close to his eyes. Any one of these could be due to poor habit formation, but the eyesight should be considered suspect and examined accordingly.

For those children who recognise letters, a Snellen's chart may be used. For the younger child, a chart showing silhouettes of familiar objects is a good guide. The images decrease in size from the top line to the bottom. All boys should be screened for colour blindness. In any type of vision testing, we must take into account the sociability of the child and his willingness to co-operate. Also his intellectual skill and previous experience will affect, for good or ill, the result of the test.

CO-ORDINATION

Our fine manipulative skill, enhanced by our complex vision, has given us the ability to construct the most complicated and efficient machines to create some of the most beautiful artistic works and excel at written communication. The acquired skill of hands and the excellent visual equipment with which we are endowed together provide the means of exploring a vast number of objects and situations and therefore form a tremendous function in learning.

Hand/eye co-ordination (eyes and hands working together) comes about through growth and maturity. At birth, the pupils react to light i.e. they will contract when a small pencil light comes near to the eye. The child will blink at a sudden sound. His eyes are usually closed when he is resting, but if we lift him to a vertical posture, he will open his eyes. It seems he has already learned that it is practical to have one's eyes open when in a standing position!

As the child learns to control his neck muscles and turn his head it is noticeable that he is attracted by light and will stare fixedly at sources of blank light e.g. a window.

Very soon he will gaze at his mother's face when she feeds him. It is vital to the communication between a mother and her child that she returns this visual attention and gives him her full concentration during these very intimate moments. Her reward will come when her smile is acknowledged and returned. The first smile is seen at around the 6th week of life. For the 1st time he fixes both eyes on her face and responds with a smile. Not entirely a visual response, but it is clearly seen as an important sign of developing visual ability. From here on we see the early development of hand/eye co-ordination. He becomes increasingly more wakeful and alert. By 3–4 months he will hold his head erect and look around. If we stimulate his vision with a dangling toy he will converge both eyes and follow its movement both horizontally and vertically (**convergence**).

He begins to learn about his body; he discovers he has fingers and his hands which were previously closed begin to open and close. He clasps and unclasps his hands, pressing the palms together as he does so. He will now accept a rattle placed in his hand, but his movements are aimless and, unless supervised, he will bang it against his face.

These early manipulations take place in the mid-line, above his body and close to his line of vision. The movements of his fingers attract his eyes and he examines them closely. This is termed 'hand regard'.

Approaching 6 months he will raise his arms, shoulders and head to be lifted. He is extremely curious now and will soon become bored if there is nothing to see. He likes to be propped where he can watch trees moving, traffic passing, but mostly the coming and going of his favourite adults. He welcomes the preparation of his feeds and will pat with apparent affection the breast or bottle while he sucks. When being fed with a spoon he will reach with both hands for the spoon. If he is offered a cup he will attempt to hold the sides so the cup should be designed with two handles.

Close observation of his hands at this time will show that he grasps with the whole hand any object placed before him and brings it to his mouth for further investigation (bi-manual approach – palmar grasp). He has become an expert at working both eyes together and a squint is now an abnormality.

With the advent of crawling, any colourful object will encourage him to move towards it. He will begin to follow a moving object such as a colourful ball. His approach will now be single handed and it will be observed that he pats the ball with

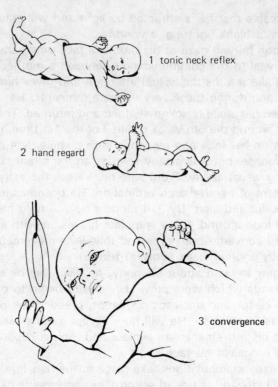

1 tonic neck reflex

2 hand regard

3 convergence

Fig 5.2   development of hand/eye co-ordination

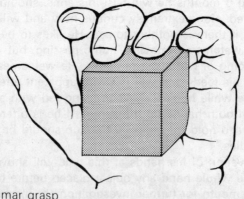

Fig 5.3   palmar grasp

the palm of his hand and, provided it is of suitable size, will grasp it crudely using his fingers. His thumb plays little part in the mechanism of grasp at this age and until he learns to bring his thumb in apposition to his fingers his grasp will remain crude and ineffectual. Most babies at this age will use both hands

Fig 5.4

grasp using fingers   pincer grasp

equally well, but we commonly see the beginnings of hand preference developing and observe that he frequently uses one hand more than the other (**handedness**).

He will accept 2 small bricks one after the other and gain great pleasure from the noise of banging them together in an imitation of the adult. Where releasing an object was previously involuntary and due to waning of interest, by 10–11 months he has acquired the skill of voluntary release and will give up a cube on request.

The skill of release becomes quite forceful very quickly and at this age we find him casting his toys out of the pram as often as an accommodating adult will retrieve and replace them. A great game, tiring the adult long before the baby. If a toy is not retrieved, he will look for it and verbalise his desires loudly and at length.

By the end of his 1st year, thumb and forefinger are brought in apposition and we find him approaching objects with an extended poking forefinger and picking up the tiniest crumb quite skilfully with thumb and forefinger (pincer grasp). Given access to

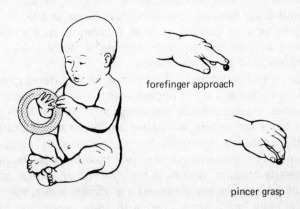

forefinger approach

pincer grasp

Fig 5.5

bricks and with an adult to demonstrate their building potential, he will construct a tower of 3 bricks.

As we have seen previously, the child appears unable to cope with more than one major skill and we find that during his 2nd year his fine skills progress more slowly than in the past year and language goes ahead. Given a thick crayon he will revert to holding it with palmar grasp, usually mid-shaft, and he will execute a to and fro scribble. He will point to familiar pictures in a book and turn its pages, demonstrating as he does so a distinct preference for one hand. He loves to help with feeding himself, using his fingers, but given a spoon he would probably go hungry. The successful use of a spoon is a very sophisticated manoeuvre requiring delicate movements of wrist and fingers and, because most babies invert the spoon in their early attempts, more food reaches the baby's bib and lap than enters his mouth.

The end of his 2nd year will see his construction ability extending to a tower of 6 or more bricks. He holds a crayon with the preferred hand and he will spontaneously make circles, to and fro scribble and dots. At this age, his creative ability is best expressed using his hands and he will experiment with paint using his whole hand and fingers.

Within this next year, many children will attend a nursery school or playgroup. Here he will find all the basic play materials e.g. paint, clay, water, wet and dry sand, dough and bricks, and adults who will direct his experience of these materials to useful purpose as his intellect and development dictate. With opportunity to explore first the properties of these materials and later what he can do with them, his manipulative skills will increase. He will find more demanding playthings e.g. interlocking bricks and rods, beads and strings, jigsaws, posting boxes and other manipulative toys, all designed to increase his fine skills and his knowledge of the world around him. Through practice of this kind, he will come to undress and dress himself, managing fastenings and laces, he will learn to turn taps on and off, to flush a lavatory, turn a door handle, feed himself and generally acquire those fine skills which will ultimately lead to independence.

Through finger plays and action songs he will develop a flexibility and strength in his fingers which will aid the control of paint brushes, crayons, modelling tools; all of which form a very important basis for writing skills later on. Given the opportunity and suitable materials, the pre-schooler will learn to manipulate scissors and his entire creative play will take on more recognisable form. His early attempt to draw a man will be an extension of the strokes he has already mastered e.g. circles and single strokes. The typical early 'man' has a head with limbs protruding from it.

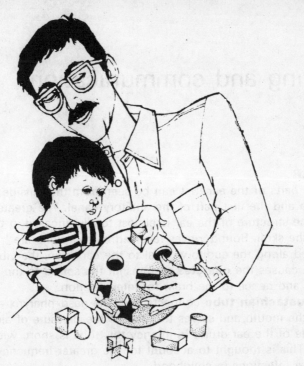

Fig 5.6   '... playthings ... designed to increase his fine skills ...'

Great detail is given to the face he paints, which may indicate the importance that the face has for the child. A body and neck will come as skill and observation increase.

Most children entering school are sufficiently independent to cope with hair brushing, teeth cleaning, dressing and undressing, managing the lavatory routine and handwashing. He may cope with a knife and fork, but he will use them with elbows sticking out and will be approaching 6 or 7 years of age before he can manage to cut anything but the softer foods.

6
Hearing and communication

THE EAR

The only parts of the ear that can be seen from the outside are the pinna and the first part of the auditory canal. The greater part of the structure of the ear is almost totally encased in the base of the skull. Sound waves received by the pinna are conducted along the auditory canal to the ear drum, the vibration of which causes the **ossicles** to transmit the sound to the **cochlea** and hence to the brain for interpretation.

The **Eustachian tube** connects with the naso-pharynx at the back of the mouth and serves to equalise the pressure of air on either side of the ear drum. In infancy this tube is short, wide and straight. This is thought to account for the greater frequency of middle ear infections in childhood.

The ear is also concerned with balance. As a result of various stimuli received from the eyes, the hands and other surfaces of the body, fluid in the **semi-circular canals** is displaced, causing the nerve cells around to pick up and transmit messages to the brain concerning the position of the body relative to its environment.

Hearing appears to be acute at birth, and within a few days of birth the baby will be startled by a loud noise or soothed by a comforting voice. From these early days the young baby should be exposed to the normal sounds in his environment e.g. speech, the vacuum cleaner, the telephone, the door bell and all the other sounds created by a normal household. From this plethora of sounds the child learns to identify specific sounds and to discriminate between human speech, music, household noises etc, and gradually his response to each is modified with experience.

This development of aural discrimination is vital to the development of speech. When we consider the subtle differences between sounds e.g. *f* and *th*, *p* and *b*, *m* and *n*, it is hardly surprising that the child may experience difficulty in detecting the difference and therefore make mistakes in his speech. Take this example of a young child approaching 3 years of age attempting a well known nursery rhyme:

'Little blue peep,
Come blow up your sheep,
Where's the little boy who looks after the sheep?
He's dragging his tail behind him.'

Here, we see a child who has learned the rhythm, some of the words, but has made some delightful confusions. Some degree of perception has taken place but his memory and the motor skills required to make certain sounds have let him down. Other typical

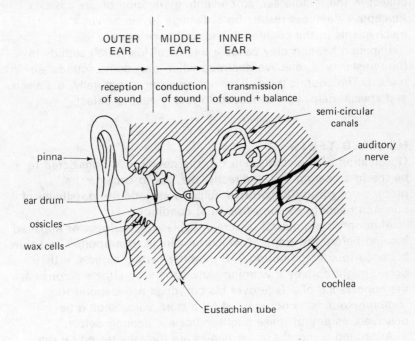

OUTER EAR	MIDDLE EAR	INNER EAR
reception of sound	conduction of sound	transmission of sound + balance

- semi-circular canals
- auditory nerve
- pinna
- ear drum
- ossicles
- wax cells
- cochlea
- Eustachian tube

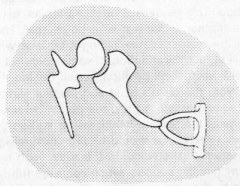

ossicles enlarged to show articulation

Fig 6.1   the ear

errors are 'gog' for 'dog', 'babbit' for 'rabbit', and only careful listening to the child when he speaks and guidance in the production of the correct sound will determine whether this is a perceptual or a motor difficulty.

Sometimes, due to repeated ear infection and the resulting damage to the hearing mechanism, a child may suffer from conductive or perceptive deafness. Conductive deafness is due to interference with the transmission of sound waves and is often due to a mechanical defect in the middle ear. Viscous mucus may collect in the middle ear, so preventing vibration of the ossicles. Perceptive deafness results from damage to the nervous mechanisms in the cochlea or the **auditory nerve.**

Impaired hearing may cause a degree of loss of all sounds in the register or a selective deafness when only some sounds are missed. The sounds missed are not reproduced naturally in speech and special help will be needed to rectify such a defect.

HEARING TESTS

Observation of the startle reflex in the newborn is considered to be the first hearing test. Indirectly, the test to exclude the presence of **phenylketonuria** helps to exclude the possibility of impaired hearing resulting from that condition.

Although it is unusual to screen babies for deafness or impaired hearing before the stage at which he can sit unsupported and turn his head to sound (around 7–8 months) certain signals, if they occur, might convey a warning. Any baby who shows surprise at the appearance of a face over his cot, does not respond to soothing sounds, is not startled by a stern voice should be observed, as any of these might indicate a hearing defect.

At around 8 months, most babies are formally tested by the distraction method. This requires 2 qualified adults, usually health visitors, plus the mother, if the test is to be reliable. The baby is supported on the mother's knee, facing a table at which one health visitor will attract his attention to some colourful playthings. The second health visitor will position herself behind the baby, about 2 metres from the child's head and parallel with his ear. When the baby is engrossed in play, the object is removed and at that precise moment the second health visitor will softly call his name. A satisfactory response would be prompt turning of the head and localisation of the voice. In this way, each ear is tested using a variety of familiar sounds which span the full range of tones. Response to the spoken voice is of greatest importance.

By the time the child is 2 years old, co-operation testing may be possible. As its title suggests, this form of testing requires the co-operation of the child and its success is therefore dependent upon his degree of sociability, his mood on the day, and his intelligence. A selection of small toys e.g. a tiny doll, a bath, doll's house furniture, farmyard animals etc is placed on a table at which the child and the tester sit. The child is then asked to perform certain simple tasks e.g. 'put the baby in the bath', 'place the chair at the table'. The tester varies the vocabulary, the tone and the volume of speech and notes the child's response. After this, the emergence of a satisfactory vocabulary and language development is a fair guide to the integrity of the hearing.

In some areas, all school children between 6 and 8 years of age are pure tone tested using an audiometer. This piece of apparatus conveys pure tone signals to the child via headphones. The child is required to press a button every time a tone is detected. Each ear is tested and a record of his responses is charted. Repeat tests will be made on any child who does not respond at a satisfactory level.

Sometimes a poor result can be due to something simple like a cold at the time of testing, but more serious conditions must be eliminated or diagnosed and the appropriate care and treatment implemented immediately.

CRYING

Crying in the newborn baby has many functions. The exercise value has been mentioned. The first cry is specially significant because it is an indication of lung function. To emit a loud cry, the child must first have inhaled a reasonable amount of air which, in forcing out, causes the noise we call crying. Obviously the noise is designed to draw attention to the baby's need for something. That something may be one or more of many desires. Very soon a new mother learns to discriminate the cry of her baby from a number of babies crying at the same time. As she gets to know her baby she learns to recognise the hunger cry, the tired cry, the cry of pain, and the cry that says 'I want your company'. She will also observe that her baby does not shed tears when he cries until he is about a month old. This may be why the cry is not taken seriously on occasions. Frequently we hear mothers say, 'There are no tears', in a rather scoffing tone which appears to imply that the absence of tears indicates an absence of need.

In recent years most child care experts have agreed that response to the cry and satisfying the need cause the cry to cease. We do not 'spoil' babies by helping them, we encourage their growth and development. Those babies whose needs are met as promptly as possible cry less.

In the past it was believed that crying was 'good' for a baby. It caused him to fully expand his lungs. That may well be valid to a degree, but the adverse effects of prolonged crying outweigh any good it may do. He will become so distressed that composure is difficult, he will swallow large quantities of air and the distension of his stomach will cause pain. Exhaustion will overtake him and he may fall asleep, but this tends to be a fitful sleep punctuated by sobbing.

Most adults expect babies to cry, but if the crying exceeds their expectation they become over anxious, over protective or ignore him and hope he will go away. Perhaps they think he is over demanding. This implies that the child has reasoning ability and is deliberately trying to annoy.

The best antidote to crying is often the human voice and handling. That, of course, will not satisfy the hungry baby for long; but when all else fails, talk to him. Hold him tight, close to the face, let him feel the soothing vibrations as you coo in his ear. Quiet can be unnerving for many people. Perhaps this is the case in a new baby who prior to birth was surrounded by sounds. The womb must be a very noisy place, situated as it is near to the aorta which emits a gentle rhythmic 'swoosh' in time with the heart beat, and the bowel which is constantly gurgling.

The need to cry decreases as other forms of communication develop. Facial expressions, early verbalising, postures, gestures, all tell us a great deal. There is a direct relationship between decreasing crying and increasing language development. The total body movement is replaced by a specific response.

Throughout the pre-school years, despite a blossoming vocabulary, spontaneous crying will occur until the child learns that crying in most instances is destructive, he becomes more upset, whereas making a specific request is more conducive to satisfaction of his needs.

Naturally, he will cry when he is physically or emotionally hurt. This is a safety valve which brings relief from shock or tension and resolves when he is comforted. The ill child will cry because illness brings apprehension, or worse, fear. The tired child will cry. He's allowed to, isn't he? We are all fragile when we are tired.

Crying can bring out the worst in people. We often deal with it badly due to the irritation caused by the noise and the frustration of helplessness.

DEVELOPMENT OF LANGUAGE

It is accepted now that human babies have an innate potential for speech, the development of which is dependent upon the integrity of the hearing and speech structures and maturation of the brain and nervous system. Speech becomes a social activity which is encouraged by a warm, affectionate atmosphere, motivation and guidance in the learning of language.

There are 3 stages of development through which a child must pass successfully in order to learn the skills of language. These are:

1 the early communication of infancy
2 speech (the use of words)
3 language (words said with meaning and later used in sentences).

At all stages of life, but particularly in childhood, language is used in conjunction with many forms of non-verbal communication which are used to compensate for language deficiency or to enhance the effect of the spoken word. The child or adult without speech uses these mechanisms to communicate very successfully. Occasionally due to mood, emotional upset or personality, speech may be withheld and communication takes place through non-verbal means. These include facial expression, visual engagement, gesture, posture, skin colour changes, crying, touch, emotionally charged noises, laughter, tantrums, and creative activities such as painting, modelling, drama, mime, writing, music and dance.

In general, many of the very physical forms of communication decrease as language ability becomes more proficient. In this respect language conforms to 2 principles of development:

a) generalised activity is replaced by a specific response
b) development is dependent upon maturation of the nervous system.

Parts of the body concerned with speech

1 ear – reception and transmission of sound

2 brain – interpretation of sounds heard, memory, nervous stimulation of the mechanical apparatus of speech

3 tongue, lips, palate and teeth and vocal chords – provide variation of sound

4 lungs, muscles of the chest wall and diaphragm – control the volume of air expelled and vary the intensity of speech sounds.

Due to irregular rates of maturation, the tongue, lips and larynx become active before the speech centre in the brain and the nervous mechanisms. This explains why a baby of 6–8 weeks onwards will engage in 'vocal gymnastics' i.e. gurgling, cooing, blowing bubbles and babbling. All of which provide very important pre-speech practice.

During this stage the child is learning control of the tongue, lips etc. The vibrations in his throat give him pleasurable sensations and he repeats the game, encouraged by the participation of the adult who coos and babbles back to him. This affectionate response elicited from favourite adults adds the social and emotional dimensions to speech development.

Developmental patterns

Sound is made by air expelled from the lungs causing the vocal chords to vibrate. The tone is determined by the throat and mouth. Later, these sounds are formed into letters and words by the tongue, palate, lips and teeth. Air drawn into the lungs must pass gently downwards through the vocal chords if choking is to be avoided. A young baby experiences the discomfort of forceful inhalation when he cries and very quickly learns to avoid the experience.

The impulse of the caring adult to talk to the young baby during bathing, cuddling or feeding provides the child with a language model and is soon rewarded by the infant's throaty noises made in response to the adult's voice. Due to the shape of the palate and the uncontrolled expulsion of air from the lungs, many early baby sounds are explosive. Such guttural and explosive sounds are made universally, by all babies, whatever the language they will ultimately adopt.

Very soon, the baby will turn his head in response to his name, indicating a degree of comprehension developing before the ability to use words. His repertoire is largely vowel sounds initially, but an extension of the sucking movements and the presence of teeth soon give rise to the appearance of 'mama' and 'dada', which in the early days have no relevance to the person but are merely experimentation with the vocal mechanisms. The tongue is attached to the floor of the mouth by a fold of skin called the frenum. In infancy, the tongue is short from front to back and many sounds will not be possible for the child until the tongue has lengthened and grown well beyond the frenum. Then, with the greater mobility afforded, the tongue can assist with the more sophisticated sounds.

A little later, the babble adopts a rhythm of speech and the child begins to imitate sounds he has heard. This is the stage at which speech development may become arrested for the deaf child, who because he cannot hear cannot imitate. By the end of the 1st year of life the baby is on the first rung of the speech ladder. His behaviour shows that he can understand more than he can say. He will comply with simple requests, especially if they are accompanied by a particular tone of voice (No!), facial expression or gesture in preparation for some activity such as going out.

Repetitious baby words are frowned upon by some, and yet they have a place. The more practice a baby gets, the quicker his language will develop. Many so-called baby words are **onomatopoeic** and therefore assist with meaning, others make use of the early consonant sounds e.g. 'moo cow', 'bow wow', 'gee gee', 'bye bye'. Most children adapt to the use of the correct word in due course.

The baby is now entering the stage when he uses the correct word for the right object and with understanding. This stage is often reached between 12 and 15 months but may be delayed if the baby is still organising his walking skill. The repetition of certain sounds in the presence of specific objects helps the child to make association between sounds and objects or people. With encouragment and guidance, the child will repeat such sounds in the presence of the correct object or person. This development can only progress at the rate that memory and reasoning progress.

During the 2nd year, his vocabulary of nouns will expand but, on occasions, he will be frustrated by his inability to find the right word, so he will point and say 'Err!' Having grasped the rhythms and tones of speech, but not yet a full range of words, the infant will indulge in scribble talk — strings of random sounds having no obvious meaning, but odd words are decipherable. At this time the small child is experimenting with the questioning tone, the command tone and other inflections that will ultimately assist his language to be more meaningful and interesting to hear. Children at this stage are sensitive to emotions expressed in the voice and will attempt to imitate.

Early attempts at sentence structure are a great source of enjoyment, not only to the child who can now really begin to communicate verbally, but also to those around him, since some very amusing errors in pronunciation and word order (syntax) occur. 'Me do it' sometimes means 'I want to do it', equally it could mean 'You do it'. The intonation rather than the correct use of words conveys the intended meaning.

Concept formation and language develop hand in hand and are complementary. The correct use of 'me' and 'I' will only come with guidance from those around and the child's developing awareness of himself. The concept of time is a very difficult one for young children to understand, but long before he can tell the time, general concepts of past, present and future are evident in his correct use of tenses. Experiments in this area can be great fun!

> Small child: 'I went to the park today.'
> Adult: 'Did you? When?' (meaning 'at what time?').
> Small child: 'Yesterday.'

Plurals are used naturally most of the time by the child who hears them used and he avoids the errors of 'foots', 'mans', 'tooths'. However, even the child who speaks in these terms has grasped that the addition of an 's' makes some words plural.

Sentences lengthen now, but are often incomplete and frequently joined by 'and' to relate an event or story. It is at this stage that those around must be patient and resist the temptation to interrupt or finish the sentence because speech is one way in which the child forms thoughts. Initially, he organises his thoughts in words. When solving a problem at play he will often give a commentary

Fig 6.2 '... talk to him.'

74

on his activities. He asks himself questions; and often answers them, too.

The young child seems to adopt 3 levels of speech: the speech he uses to think; the speech he uses with other children; and even the different speech he uses with adults. In conversation with other children he often imitates their use of words, tries new and unfamiliar words that they use and may also copy any mistakes he hears. When talking to adults, he may produce complex words used through imitation, and out of context.

The rate of development from here is largely dependent upon the environment. Given a helpful language environment, the quality of a child's vocabulary and grammar will improve indefinitely. Modification will occur through education, socialisation and growing emotional control. Hopefully, every child will find pleasure in using language successfully, in listening to the human voice and sharing conversations.

A rich language environment will supply the child with a varied vocabulary, experiences to promote thought, reasoning, pleasure, the opportunity for the child to practise his developing skill, and adults around him who will make language a rewarding acquisition. As well as all this motivation, he needs guidance in the details of language techniques and, most important of all, a satisfactory model to copy.

7
Digestion

DIGESTION AND THE ENCOURAGEMENT OF A HEALTHY APPETITE

The digestive canal is a tube which starts in the mouth and continues downwards to the pharynx, the oesophagus or gullet, the stomach, the small and large intestines. Along its length it changes in size and structure according to the particular function it has to perform. It is well supplied with muscle tissue which keeps the contents moving in an onward direction. The ripple of contraction passing through the muscle coat of the digestive canal is called peristalsis. At certain points e.g. at the inlet and outlet to the stomach, small purse string muscles control the flow. The canal has a very efficient blood supply which nourishes it and also conveys away nutritious substances for use in other parts of the body.

Accessory structures include the teeth, tongue and cheeks. These reduce food to a state in which it may be swallowed. Saliva from the salivary glands moistens the food to ease its passage and also contains an enzyme which begins the digestive process.

The stomach is a widely dilated structure which receives food that has been swallowed and churns it, mixing it with gastric juices and reducing it to a liquid state.

In the abdomen, other glands supply different enzymes which are specific in their action of breaking down certain foods: these are the liver and pancreas which pour their secretions into the first part of the small intestine.

Absorption is the process by which nutritious substances in a dissolved state pass through the wall of the small intestine to enter the blood stream and be transported away. By the time the residue reaches the end of the small intestine, most of what can be used by the body has been removed. All that remains which is vital to life is water and this will be removed by the large intestine.

The end result of digestion is waste matter which is excreted as faeces by the lower end of the large colon.

In order to use the absorbed substances, we need an adequate supply of oxygen. Nutrition depends upon a process known as 'metabolism', which is the result of the seven processes listed below:

1 *ingestion* — the intake of food
2 *digestion* — the breakdown of food to a soluble state
3 *absorption* — the 'pick up' of digested nutrients
4 *circulation* — the transport of digested nutrients
5 *respiration* — the supply of oxygen
6 *oxidation* — the process by which nutrients are used to build tissues and create energy
7 *excretion* — the removal of waste products.

THE DIGESTIVE TRACT OF A BABY

We must never make the mistake of assuming that a baby is merely a small adult. This is especially important in the matter of feeding him. His needs are different and his apparatus for dealing with food is far from mature.

At birth, his body makes all the necessary enzymes for the digestion of protein, fat, carbohydrate. He can absorb mineral salts and vitamins. His fluid requirement per kilo of body weight is greater than the adult's. The flow of saliva is sparse at birth and therefore the enzyme it contains which is necessary for the breakdown of carbohydrate is limited. In the stomach, the acid content is less. **Pepsin,** which aids the digestion of protein, is present and gradually increases in quantity during the early months of life. The baby's ability to deal with carbohydrate is immature. Fat is difficult to digest at any age, but especially so in infancy.

The essence of success lies in the preparation of food for the young child. Initially, he can only digest milk, and then only if it is breast milk or modified cows' milk. He has well developed rooting and sucking reflexes which will enable him to acquire his milk, but the swallowing reflex is only stimulated by the presence of the nipple or teat at the back of his throat.

If we observe him closely, we will notice that around the 3rd or 4th month the flow of saliva increases to the extent that he cannot swallow as quickly as it is produced and he dribbles. This is often interpreted as the onset of 'teething' but is, in fact, an indication that the digestive mechanism is maturing and he can take more complex foods: complex, that is, in content. The texture of the food must be **puréed** in order that he may swallow it. At this early stage, food placed in the front of the mouth will be pushed out due to the immature action of the tongue. Any foods offered by spoon must be placed well to the back of the mouth.

Voluntary swallowing, more sophisticated movements of the tongue and dentition will follow soon and can be clearly observed. This heralds the beginning of the child's ability to manage foods of a coarser texture. The ability to masticate successfully will not occur until the molars have erupted. Only then can the child bite and grind and mix his food with saliva ready for swallowing.

The need for food causes hunger pains, due to increased peristalsis in the stomach. This is uncomfortable and causes the baby to cry. Milk entering the stomach will make the pain go away and the baby will become composed. Development of a healthy appetite is based upon this sequence of discomfort, food and relief and is influenced by the senses of smell, taste and touch.

We know why he eats, but why does he stop eating? Several factors are involved. He may become tired due to the effort of sucking. This might indicate that small amounts more frequently are best for him. Filling of the stomach will make it comfortably distended and he recognises that he has had suffecent for the moment. If the food is satisfactory in content, his blood sugar and blood fat levels will increase and his metabolic mechanisms will control his intake.

Feeding healthy babies and young children should not become a problem. The baby's only difficulty is that he has no ability to fend for himself in the early days and depends entirely upon the caring adult to supply his needs. In order to do this, the required nutritional knowledge can be gained from many excellent sources, such as the well-baby clinic, the G P, health visitor or a variety of books and leaflets. The acquisition of basic knowledge is just the beginning.

Successful feeding habits depend upon co-operation with the baby. Learn to recognise the hunger cry, supply suitable food and allow the baby control over what he eats. It is vital to foster an enjoyment of eating. He must feel comfortable and secure while he feeds. Breast feeding is ideal for many reasons, not least of which is the fact that the baby must be held close to the mother's body while he is nursed.

Just as we take care to tempt our own palate, we must observe preferences as they develop in the child and offer a variety of foods from which selections may be made. We must also observe the young child's growing independence and take account of those periods when his appetite fluctuates. There will be a natural decrease in demand when his growth rate slows.

The greatest hindrance to successful eating is anxiety. The child is not born with any reservations regarding food or eating, but he will easily detect any anxiety in the adult and internalise this emotion. Digestion is inhibited by stress and may even cause the child to vomit. The greatest force for good appetite development is a happy relationship with those around him. Calm and peace is conducive to a rewarding experience which he will want to repeat.

Part of the child's socialisation is to adopt the eating pattern of his family. He learns quickly, his needs change and he feeds less frequently. By the time he has completed the 1st year of life he will sit at the table and take part in family meal times.

Throughout the rest of childhood, the principles remain the same. The good habits started in baby days will become established and with minor setbacks will set the pattern for life. The stomach can be comfortably filled and hunger goes away. If we overfeed, the stomach gradually becomes accustomed to being over-distended and is only satisfied when stretched. This sets a pattern of over-eating which establishes unhealthy habits and can predispose to obesity.

When food passes into the upper end of the digestive tract, the wave of muscle contraction (peristalsis) which ripples through the whole system stimulates activity at the lower end. It is not surprising then that, if we observe the feed/excretion pattern of a baby, we note that he commonly excretes faeces soon after a meal.

JAW DEVELOPMENT AND DENTITION

At birth, the lower jaw is very small and forms almost a right angle. The upper and lower jaws consist of 2 separate halves joined in the mid-line by a pad of cartilage which usually hardens by the end of the 1st year. The tooth buds are present and developing within the jaw. Development of the jaw accelerates while the primary teeth are erupting, and the pattern of the jaw is usually established within the first 3 years of life. After that, a more angular outline develops as the primary (deciduous) teeth are shed in order that secondary dentition may take place.

Growth and development of the jaw may be inadequate, resulting in an unusual pattern of eruption causing crowding (malalignment) or poor closure in the biting position (malocclusion).

Sucking at the breast and subsequent chewing exercise the muscles surrounding and supporting the jaw and stimulate circulation and growth.

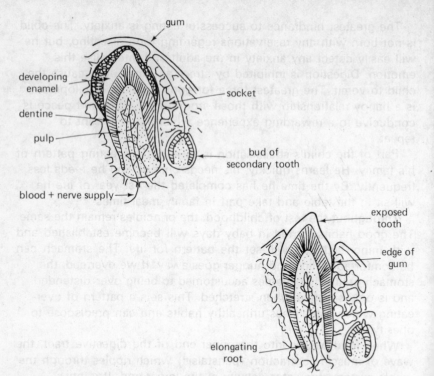

Fig 7.1   development of a tooth

Labels on the figure:
- gum
- developing enamel
- dentine
- pulp
- blood + nerve supply
- socket
- bud of secondary tooth
- exposed tooth
- edge of gum
- elongating root

If we think of Stone Age people with their very heavy bone structure and immensely powerful jaw line and we reflect on their eating habits e.g. raw meat and vegetable material we can see why they, with the same number of teeth, never suffered from malalignment and malocclusion. Similarly, the Eskimos, whose eating habits are similar, share the same design of jaw and are known not to suffer from the dental abnormalities of the more sophisticated societies. This is the price we have paid for civilisation and refined eating habits e.g. cooking, soft foods, sweets etc.

The teeth form the first part of the digestive system and, as such, their eruption is closely associated with the maturing process of the digestive tract. We have 3 types of teeth, each designed to fulfil a particular purpose: the incisors or cutting teeth, the molars or grinding teeth and the canine teeth or tearing teeth. The canine teeth are so called because they resemble the sharp pointed teeth found in the jaws of dogs and other meat eating animals who tear their food. Each of these types of teeth will appear in the jaw in good time as the child approaches the age when his digestive system can tolerate foods to be bitten, chewed and torn.

For the 40 weeks of his foetal life, nutritious substances have passed from the mother's blood via the placenta directly into the child's own circulation. At birth, or shortly afterwards, his digestion is required to work alone for the first time. Initially, this immature system can only tolerate milk, the acquisition of which requires merely strong sucking and the ability to swallow. As the child's nutritious demands increase and the digestive system matures sufficiently to tolerate biting foods, the incisor teeth start to erupt and their development is encouraged by the opportunity for biting. Similarly, at about 12–15 months the molar teeth start to erupt as the child shows signs of tolerating minced and finely chopped foods. Finally, the process is completed with the eruption of the canine teeth and final set of molars towards the end of the 2nd year of life. We commonly find that primary dentition starts at around 5–6 months and the child has a full set of 20 primary teeth at around $2\frac{1}{2}$ years. Eruption of the large molars coincides with the beginning of independence at about $2\frac{1}{2}$–3 years. This is commonly referred to as the 'negative age' because the child tests his new found independence against adult authority.

Pain experienced due to teething at this time can cause adverse reactions and an exaggeration of the negative stage e.g. the 'good as gold' baby becomes the 'troublesome 2 year old'.

Fig 7.2   teeth

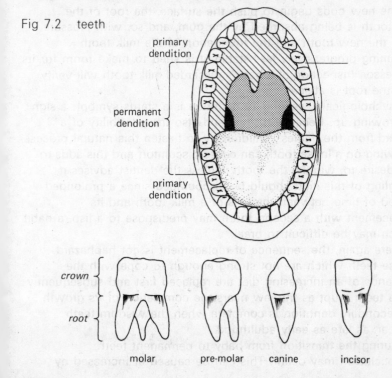

primary dentition

permanent dentition

primary dentition

crown

root

molar   pre-molar   canine   incisor

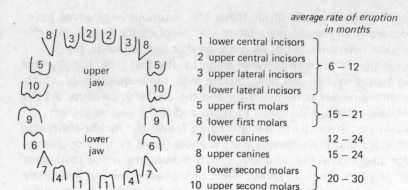

1 lower central incisors	
2 upper central incisors	
3 upper lateral incisors	6 – 12
4 lower lateral incisors	
5 upper first molars	
6 lower first molars	15 – 21
7 lower canines	12 – 24
8 upper canines	15 – 24
9 lower second molars	
10 upper second molars	20 – 30

Fig 7.3   primary dentition chart

As a milestone, teething is useless. In common with other areas of development, the rate of dentition varies from child to child, and whilst the time of eruption is relatively unimportant, the correct sequence of eruption is desirable for good jaw formation and the spacing of the teeth. One common cause of late eruption is prematurity.

Eruption of the permanent teeth commences around $5\frac{1}{2}$–6 years. As the new buds begin to push the surface, the root of the first tooth is being absorbed by the gum, and so, with pressure from the new tooth and the foundation of the milk tooth becoming progressively less stable, it is shed to make room for its successor. Inspection of a baby's discarded milk tooth will verify that the root is absent.

Psychologically, secondary dentition is a status symbol: a sign of growing up. Because of this, and also the possibility of a reward from the 'fairies', children try to hasten this natural process. Chewing on a loose tooth can cause discomfort and this adds to the desire to 'wiggle' the tooth. Unless the dentist advises it, wiggling of this kind should be discouraged since a prolonged period of time between the loss of a milk tooth and its replacement with a second tooth may predispose to a lisp, a habit which may be difficult to break.

Here again, the sequence of replacement is not haphazard. Those teeth which are not strong enough to cope with the demands of an increasing diet are replaced first and subsequently extra teeth erupt as the jaw nears the completion of its growth.

Secondary dentition is complete when the wisdom teeth appear, as late as early adulthood.

During the transition from baby to permanent teeth, malocclusion may occur. This can be caused or increased by thumb sucking, mouth breathing, pressure on the chin e.g. sleeping on tummy, tongue biting. Many malocclusions correct themselves. Occasionally it is necessary to consult an **orthodontist** since malocclusion not only affects appearance and speech but also inhibits satisfactory chewing, which results in poor digestion.

'Teething' is a natural process, which in common with other natural processes is not without discomfort. The baby may be fretful, restless, temporarily off his food to an extent that medical help may be required. However, 'teething' produces only teeth. Diarrhoea or bronchitis is not part of the process. It is often noticed that the child's stools are more fluid at this time, which may be explained by the extra saliva produced due to the general irritation in the mouth. A mild cough is not uncommon, which can also be attributed to excess saliva — saliva which is produced at such a rate that the child dribbles and is unable to fully control any which collects at the back of the throat. Teething appears to lower the resistance to infection, possibly due to loss of sleep and appetite, and a cold often adds to the child's discomfort at this time.

The avoidance of hard foods, extra fluids, warmth and most of all comfort will help to soothe these troublesome symptoms. Teething creams and jellies may have a place, but the astringent effect of fresh lemon juice, gently applied to inflamed gums, will soothe any soreness.

DENTAL CARE

The child's dental care begins in pregnancy, with the mother supplying the nutritious substances necessary for tooth development — vitamin D, calcium and other minerals. This is continued after birth in the child's own diet.

Breast feeding requires greater jaw action than bottle feeding and is therefore conducive to good jaw development. Subsequent activity is provided in chewing hard foods, which should be included in every child's diet.

Most people are informed of the connection between sweets and dental decay, but an awareness of the danger to teeth of cough syrups, vitamin syrups and antibiotics is desirable. The prolonged presence of sugars in the mouth causes acid formation which can destroy the enamel and give rise to invasion by organisms and subsequent decay. Antibiotics and cough syrup given at night should be followed by water or mouth wash.

Cleaning should begin as soon as 2 adjacent teeth erupt. Two teeth lying together provide a gap in which food can be trapped and decay can start. A very soft brush used in baby days to massage the gums will increase the blood supply to the teeth and gums, thereby helping to maintain their healthy condition and guard against infection. Initially, cleansing by the mother is done using a soft baby-sized toothbrush or a small piece of damp cotton wool mounted on a smooth orange stick. In this way, the mother is introducing the beginning of a health habit which the child will take over himself. Toothpaste is not important, initially, but when the time comes it is wise to choose a pleasant flavoured toothpaste, preferably containing fluoride, and provide a small brush with which to apply it.

The young child should be introduced to the habit of dental inspection by attending with the mother as a baby. By the age of about $2\frac{1}{2}$ years the dentist will usually let the child sit in the chair and merely have his teeth inspected. Once a relationship has developed, the child may have his teeth polished just to get used to having instruments in his mouth. Some dentists provide fluoride painting or coating of each new tooth as it erupts as part of their preventive work. In this way the baby will become accustomed to the strangeness of waiting rooms, antiseptic smells, white coats. Whether or not the child should be present when the mother has treatment is a matter for the dentist to decide in the light of the mother's feelings. A mother who is frightened in the dentist's chair will convey her fear to the child.

Visits to the dentist should gradually become a normal part of the child's life. An outing that requires no special emphasis, no bribes, no treats, no threats. A child is not born with a fear of dentists. We can create fear by showing our own fears and create anxiety which might otherwise never develop.

We can help to establish the habits of dental care by example, particularly in the demonstration of the correct technique of brushing and adequate rinsing. We must provide the implements and facilities with which to do the job: a brush, toothpaste, access to water and a sink which can be reached. In the absence of these provisions e.g. in a playgroup or nursery school, we must ensure a supply of drinking water, especially after meals, or a piece of raw apple or carrot, for snacks at morning and afternoon breaks.

Our supervision of cleaning after meals if possible, but especially at night, is most important. Showing or explaining once is not enough. We must remind and remind and remind again to establish the formation of this habit. It is necessary to show an interest in well cared for teeth and praise early efforts at independence. For several years it will be necessary for the adult to check that the cleaning technique is satisfactory.

The benefits of well developed jaws and teeth lie in the confidence which comes from a pleasant appearance, the absence of infection in the mouth and stomach, the absence of unpleasant breath. Satisfactory chewing aids complete digestion. Lastly, satisfactory speech is more likely in the absence of dental abnormality.

8
Excretion

BOWEL CONTROL

The colon, or large bowel, begins at the lower right part of the abdomen, goes up the right side, passes across to the left and then down into the rectum. It has 3 functions:

1 *mechanical mixture of its contents* — by involuntary muscle action
2 *absorption of fluids* — thereby making the contents progressively drier as they complete their journey
3 *elimination of useless residue.*

It would be unreasonable to expect that a baby, born with the ability to feed and use nutritious substances, would be unable to excrete useless residue. Inborn mechanisms exist to deal with this aspect of survival. At regular periods, stimulated by increased peristalsis which results from the presence of food in the upper end of the digestive canal, faecal matter slumps in a mass into the lower end of the colon. The pressure produced causes stretching of the colon and rectum, and by reflex, initially, the tummy muscles contract, the anus relaxes and waste matter is excreted.

If we observe a young baby during this process we see that the discomfort of this fullness in the colon disturbs his repose. He fusses, he strains and then he relieves himself. We are then left in no doubt about his comfort and apparent sense of achievement. He relaxes and a serene expression passes over his face. From this we conclude that the process of excretion is pleasurable.

In order for this vital function to develop into a healthy, but later controlled, habit it is imperative that we do not interfere with the pleasure of the action by giving him foods that will put strain on this mechanism, limit his fluid intake, inhibit exercise or adopt a strict toilet training regime. Rather, we feed him according to his needs, ensure satisfactory fluid balance and exercise and co-operate with him over the practice of using a pot.

With maturity of the nervous system and relaxed practice, in his own time he will come to recognise the signals of fullness, and voluntary control will override the reflex action.

Breast fed babies often pass stools once a day or even once every 2 days, but due to the lack of waste in breast milk and the constituents of breast milk, the stools are never hard and dry. When artificial milks are used they produce harder stools and more of them. It is in this situation that we must observe the pattern of excretion closely for signs of constipation.

It is never possible to train a child in this respect. All we can do, through correctly managed practice, is show him the social ways we expect of him later in life i.e. that a lavatory (initially a potty) is the place in which this process is performed. The formula for success is simple if the process is treated as part of the child's routine, just as feeding and sleeping are routine and no special emphasis is applied.

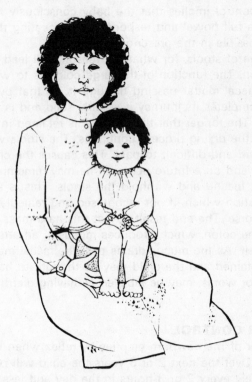

Fig 8.1   '... the completion of a pleasurable experience.'

As soon as a mother recognises from her baby's behaviour that excretion is likely it is reasonable to put the baby on a pot. This commonly occurs soon after feeds and so 'potting' in the early days is performed on the mother's lap and is therefore associated with love, security and the completion of a pleasurable experience.

87

Some mothers attempt a process known as conditioning the reflex. A conditioned reflex is one that operates in response to a given cue. In this case, the reflex to be conditioned is the expulsion of faeces. The baby may learn to empty his bowel at the feeling of the pot on his bottom. It must be stressed that he is not in control of the process. This response is merely a step along the way.

Babies vary greatly in the time at which they are ready to understand this process. It implies habit formation and maturity of the brain and nervous system. It seldom happens before 10–12 months and often takes much longer. The beginning of voluntary release of stools tends to coincide with voluntary manual release of an object given to the child to hold.

Bowel control implies that the baby consciously recognises the feeling of a full bowel and responds by evacuating the bowel as soon as possible in the prescribed place.

Retention of stools, for whatever reason, will lead to constipation. The function of the large colon is to withdraw water from the faecal matter passing through it, so that by the time this material completes its journey it is fairly solid and is moulded by the colon. The longer that this material is retained in the colon, the longer the drying process continues. The stools will ultimately become hard and difficult to pass. This causes the child discomfort and on a future occasion he may remember that unpleasant feeling and withhold the stools. This is a serious case of constipation which, if not recognised and remedied, can only become worse. The end result is that this hard mass irritates the lining of the colon, which produces mucus in an attempt to protect itself. As the mucus drains past the faecal mass it becomes stained and the child may be thought to have had 'an accident', or worse, may be labelled as having diarrhoea.

BLADDER CONTROL

The bladder of the newborn empties by reflex when it becomes distended. Over the next 2 or 3 years the child will pass urine approximately every 2 or 3 hours in the day and less often at night. As the sensation of gradual bladder distension is more subtle and less regular than the mass movement of faecal matter in the rectum, control requires greater maturity and co-operation. Clearly, it will take longer to achieve than bowel control and is greatly influenced by hormones, nervous maturity and social and emotional factors.

The bladder fills slowly as the kidneys release urine drop by drop. Awareness of a full bladder only comes as the bladder fills and begins to become distended. The small child must learn to recognise this sensation, contain the urine until he is in the socially acceptable place for elimination and release the flow of urine once there.

A baby's fluid requirement per kilo of body weight is greater than an adult's. Added to this, his stomach and bladder are proportionately smaller. This means the frequent small intake of fluid and the frequent excretion of small quantities of waste. With growth, the baby passes greater quantities of urine less frequently because:

a) his fluid requirement decreases, therefore his feeds become larger, less frequent and progressively more solid
b) his bladder can contain more fluid and he learns to retain it longer.

Retention of urine for short periods is a social convenience. However, it would be bad habit formation to allow a child to contain his bladder for so long that he has an accident or, when he does have the opportunity for urination, it is difficult for him and less satisfying.

If the pot has been introduced during the child's 1st year for the collection of faeces and the object has become familiar, 'pot' or some other meaningful word may become part of his vocabulary. The first indication of control emerging is shown when he says 'pot' meaning 'I'm wet'. Later, he will say 'pot' when he is passing urine and later still he will say 'pot' just before he voids; just before — there is no time for delay! Babies experience a sense of urgency whilst acquiring control which may lead to accidents.

The reflex emptying of the bladder is overridden by controlling influences as the young child begins to recognise the feeling of a full bladder and associates urination with the suitable receptacle in which to perform. Later, as this child becomes progressively more engrossed in his play, he may ignore the signal of bladder distension. The busy child becomes so efficient at inhibiting this reflex that the watchful adult may need to intervene occasionally to avoid bad habit formation or an accident. Every learning child needs to be reminded at some time.

Accidents may continue into the 1st year of school. Even the most aware child will have the occasional lapse when he is busy doing something interesting or during a period of stress. Whatever the cause, it is likely to go away more quickly if the child is cleansed and made more comfortable with as little fuss as possible.

Night time control
During the early months of life the pattern of urine production

changes as the kidneys become more efficient. In addition, antidiuretic hormone liberated by the pituitary gland helps to control kidney function and decreases the rate of urine production at night.

Most healthy children develop this rhythm without difficulty and night time continence soon follows day time control. In some unfortunate children this rhythm is slower to emerge, resulting in about the same amount of urine being produced at night as in the daytime. In this case, bedwetting may be prolonged. Lack of hormone control can be a cause of nocturnal enuresis (bedwetting). Anxiety is often regarded as the cause of bedwetting, but physical causes should also be investigated and the appropriate care may then be given.

The reflex actions that bring about elimination from the bowel and bladder are not primitive reflexes that go away. Rather, in health, they appear to be suppressed by the emergence of voluntary action only to return when control is disturbed by extreme emotion, illness, unconsciousness or nerve damage.

Young children attach their own words to the passing of urine and faeces. It is important in these early stages that these words are understood by all who care for him in order that his need is recognised. Proper words can be encouraged in due course.

Security with their familiar apparatus, pot or lavatory, often causes insecurity when they are faced with an alternative. For instance, it is not uncommon for a young child who is used to a pink lavatory at home to refuse to use a white one somewhere else.

At this stage, young children show intense interest in lavatories, inspecting each new lavatory that they come across. When visiting friends of the family or in a new situation they will often ask to visit the lavatory whether or not it is needed, as if to reassure themselves that it is there when they need it and that it is acceptable. The learning child should be given the benefit of any doubt when he asks to use a lavatory until it is clear that voluntary control is established.

SKIN

We see the skin so frequently that unless there is a small blemish on the complexion or an abnormality which draws our attention to it, we tend to forget what an enormously important structure this is.

Healthy skin will protect against water loss and water penetration. It offers protection against friction and infection.

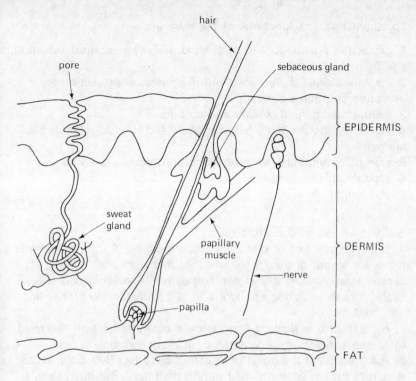

Fig 8.2   a section through the skin

Friction stimulates growth so that the outer skin surface thickens where it has to withstand wear. It provides insulation against heat loss. The **sebum** produced in the sebaceous glands flows on to the skin to maintain its elasticity and softness. Excretion of waste fluid and some mineral substances takes place due to the action of the sweat glands. The fine network of nerve endings distributed through the skin perceives touch and temperature changes. The sense of touch teaches us many of the properties of things around us; we are soothed, pleased, tickled, fearsome — according to what texture is touched. Touch warns us of danger.

The ability to adapt to temperature changes is vital to our existence and it is our skin which registers the change and to some extent effects an adaptation. It is possible to absorb substances through the skin. Ideally, these substances will be wholesome and often a treatment, but occasionally harmful substances may also be absorbed.

Last, but by no means least, important function of the skin is its ability to use the ultra-violet rays in sunlight, in conjunction with the substance **ergosterol** contained in the skin, to manufacture vitamin D.

To summarise, the functions of the skin are:

1 protection against loss of body fluid, water penetration, infection and friction
2 insulation against heat loss and in childhood protection for immature structures beneath
3 sebum maintains flexibility and softness
4 sweat glands excrete waste products and help to regulate body temperature
5 skin nerve endings perceive touch and temperature changes
6 production of vitamin D
7 absorption.

Skin changes and conditions

A 'high' colour, undue pinkness, often indicates a thin **epidermis**. If we are aware of this, it follows that these children need special care in strong sunlight and wintry weather. A paler skin is less likely to burn in strong sunlight and will withstand winter winds and cold rain.

A child who is flushed may be overheated, indicating the need for better ventilation, less clothing, or more seriously a high temperature as at the onset of infection or some other disturbance. A baby's face is often flushed during dentition. The flush may, in fact, be a blush in response to embarrassment. Occasionally, a red mottling will occur in an anxious child, but this is more commonly seen in adults.

Yellow tinges to the skin must never be ignored, since this is usually indicative of jaundice — or occasionally overindulgence in carrots!

Blueness accompanies poor circulation and, more specifically, lack of oxygen, which can be simple in origin i.e. due to cold causing the superficial blood vessels to narrow and therefore decrease the blood supply to the skin tissues. Prolonged blueness, usually most obvious around the lips, at the finger tips and the ends of the toes, may accompany a heart or lung defect and is of course not to be ignored.

The skin also varies in texture and condition. It may be moist due to excessive oil or sweat, or dry due to dehydration. These reactions made by skin to certain physical or external conditions allow us to assess the general health and wellbeing or the presence of an abnormality.

Organisms, dust, soot and debris from clothing accumulating on the skin are likely to clog the pores and give rise to unpleasant spots. Similarly, over 24 hours the skin will excrete about 1 pint of sweat and a considerable amount of sebum. If these substances are not removed, the sweat decomposes due to bacterial activity and unpleasant odours result.

When a baby is born, his skin is smeared with a natural complexion cream called vernix caseosa which has protected the skin from water surrounding him throughout the pregnancy period. It is desirable to remove this soon after birth since it will dry and become very hard, particularly in the armpits, groins, the cleft of the buttocks and behind the ears. Once hard it is extremely difficult to remove and may cause areas of soreness which may become infected.

Whilst baby bathing is commonly a daily occurrence, this is not a necessity, so long as special cleansing care is given to the skin folds and the napkin area. Probably the greatest benefit derived by the baby from the daily bath is the handling and communication he receives during the process.

Possibly the most vulnerable area of a baby's skin is the napkin area. Frequent washing, drying and application of a barrier cream will guard against napkin rash. Soreness in the napkin area may be due to a strong washing powder which has not been completely washed out. The unfortunate baby who is allowed to remain in a wet napkin may suffer a burn from the **ammonia** which forms in the napkin as the stale urine decomposes. Simple but thorough hygiene and exposure of the buttocks when the child is playing in a warm room will prevent damage of this kind.

HAIR
Each hair grows in a follicle, a tube at the bottom of which is the papilla. This is a very special structure that nourishes the growing hair and from which a new hair will grow if the old one is pulled out.

The colour of the hair is due to pigment layers in the outer skin surface. Hair colour is determined by heredity, but subject to change through development, and may become changed in colour and texture due to polluted atmospheres.

The oiliness of hair is due to the presence of the sebaceous glands, which are pouches in the wall of the follicle. These glands make sebum, a thick greasy secretion which maintains the flexibility and softness of the hair.

Each hair has a small muscle which will pull it into an erect position during sudden fear or shock. Shock may be of an emotional nature or due to changes in temperature and we say the skin is 'goosey' or we have 'goose bumps'.

There are fine hairs in most part of the body surface, the

greatest number being on the head and later appearing in the armpits and around the reproductive organs.

Growth and repair of hair

Like many other body tissues, hair passes through a cycle of growth, degeneration and loss i.e. hairs are constantly shed and replaced. In the later stages of pregnancy, the foetus is covered by fine delicate hairs known as lanugo. Mostly this is lost before birth, but may be seen on a premature baby or in some parts of the body in an immature baby e.g. face, shoulders, buttocks. After a few weeks, the lanugo is replaced by secondary hairs — also very fine and known as the vellus.

The persistent lanugo hairs on the scalp and eyebrows are shed during the 1st few months and replaced by thicker hairs. The baby of 6 months should have a shining crop of fine baby hair. The amount of hair a baby has on his head varies. It is common to see darker haired and darker skinned children with apparently more hair at birth, possibly because it is seen more clearly.

The rate at which the first hair is lost varies:

a) from child to child
b) on each child according to his favourite sleeping position
c) the length of time he spends in a lying down position since much of the hair is rubbed off and we may find bald patches occurring on one side or at the back of the head.

As the child grows through babyhood and early childhood, the hair colour and texture stabilise and the hair becomes thicker. The long hairs of the scalp are said to have a life of several years. The root gradually becomes absorbed by the follicle and the rootless hair passes up out of the shaft and is shed. A new hair is then produced by the papilla, which gradually grows up the existing shaft until it reaches the surface.

The rate of hair growth varies with the texture of the hair. Coarse hair grows faster than fine hair. It also appears that hair grows faster in summer than in winter, but growth is quite unaffected by cutting or by exposure to sunshine.

The hair insulates against loss of body heat. Bearing in mind that the head has a large surface area and a great deal of heat is lost that way, the baby's head should be kept warm until the protective, more mature hair grows. This is especially important in the case of a premature baby.

9
Emotional development

EMERGENCE OF EMOTIONS

The word 'emotion' is derived from a Latin verb, meaning to move, excite, agitate.

In order to lead a full and happy life the child must experience a variety of emotions and learn the socially acceptable ways of expressing them. At birth, inner drives such as hunger and thirst bring about excitement in the baby which we interpret as expression of a need. If that excitement is accompanied by crying, we infer that the need is pressing. When the need is satisfied, the child becomes composed and we infer that he is contented.

Within the 1st few months of life we see expression of distress due to excess warmth, cold, wind, discomfort of a soiled napkin or insecurity when being handled. With the emergence of the social smile accompanied by excitement in response to adult attention, we witness the development of delight. Happy experiences, like bathtime, evoke the same response. Curiosity is seen when the baby starts to explore his fingers, his toes, his clothing. He sees a brightly coloured toy and attempts to reach for it. He puts his fingers in his food and feels its warmth and its texture. He explores faces by poking, prodding, patting hair; spectacles have special appeal. He splashes water, rustles paper and bangs boxes. Once independent mobility is achieved his curiosity is insatiable.

Early evidence of a baby giving affection is seen just before the 1st birthday. 'Mouthing' rather than kissing of favourite adults and attention to his own mirror image shows the developing delight in physical caresses. Similar behaviour with **siblings** and soft toys may occur.

The behaviour we associate with jealousy is seldom seen before the 2nd year of life and usually takes the form of attention seeking behaviour. A mother talking to another adult while the toddler plays may find her conversation frequently interrupted by the small child pulling at her skirt and climbing on her knee. If she lifts him on to her lap and still ignores him, he will fidget or take her face firmly between his 2 hands and turn her head to face him. Even without language he is saying 'I'm here too'.

Conditioning, imitation and modelling (see Chapter 11) play a large part in moulding emotions. We can condition in a sensible and practical way for the good of the child, but must always be aware of the irrational fears that develop in childhood by the same mechanisms. Is it sensible or practical to teach a child fear of spiders, fear of birds, fear of aeroplanes, fear of lightning? He is going to grow up in a world that contains large numbers of spiders, birds, aeroplanes, and is constantly being bombarded with lightning.

Do these things often harm us? A wasp or a car, on the other hand, needs healthy respect and care. Positive moves towards dealing with hazards in life are essential and the child must learn how to cope with a world that will never be safe.

In early childhood, fear is seldom associated with threats to life or safety. An awareness of danger to life and limb does not really appear until after the child has entered school. This may be due to the inability of the young child to reason, to predict, to anticipate the effect of potentially harmful situations.

Anger is most commonly aroused by a situation that causes frustration. The favourite adult goes away, removes a meal when he wanted more, removes a toy which is constantly being banged and is causing irritation. If a toddler's developing independence is thwarted this gives rise to the tantrums associated with the 2nd and 3rd years of life. Busy adults often deny the child the time he needs because they cannot be patient; as a result, needs clash. Frustrations result from the fact that the adult always wins! Frustration of self assertion causes anger right through life. A child throws a tantrum in response to the situation; an adult has hopefully learned more sophisticated ways of channelling the emotion.

As each new emotion emerges, the child must be helped to cope with it. Distraction works well with toddlers. Explanation and teaching come later. The important role for the adult is to 'pour oil on troubled waters'; take the heat out of the situation and guide the child to healthy ways of dealing with strong feelings. This applies equally to positive and negative emotions. Just as an angry, frightened child needs help, an affectionate child must learn to give his love wisely. An elated child must learn that an excess of excitement can harm him. Curiosity must be balanced by awareness of danger and respect for other people and their property.

A child in a state of heightened emotion is comparable to a car out of control: the brakes must be applied, the car taken out of gear, the engine switched off. Then comes the time for assessment of why the car was uncontrolled and what needs to be done about it. In the same way, a child out of control emotionally needs the adult to intervene, take control when he has lost it, calm him, then teach cause and effect.

The danger to be avoided when observing the emergence of emotional development in young children is the tendency to 'read into' the behaviour something that is not there. It may be that as observers we project our own reactions into the situation and may make some inaccurate assumptions. We must look for delight, joy, affection, sympathy and give these emotions more attention than perhaps they receive in a world suffering from aggression and insecurity.

DEVELOPMENT OF EMOTIONS

Whether the ability to respond emotionally is inborn or learned is debatable. However, if we accept that feelings bring about certain forms of behaviour, we can be in no doubt that the behaviour of the newborn derives from instincts and feelings. If he is hungry or uncomfortable, he will cry; if he is about to evacuate his bowel, the feeling of fullness and discomfort will bring about fussing; when he is comfortable, well fed or being fondled, the baby will show his delight with his whole body and his facial expression will show the utmost serenity.

Perhaps then it is fair to say that certain emotions are innate, others have to be learned and, in developing emotionally, the child must learn the socially acceptable and healthy ways of expressing emotion. 'Healthy ways' implies ways in which emotions can be expressed without causing stress or physical harm.

Before we progress, let us list some of the emotions commonly felt by human beings: love, joy, curiosity, fear, worry, anxiety, anger, jealousy, sorrow, pleasure. Looking closely at this list, we see that it is possible to classify some as constructive, that is they uplift us, and some as destructive, those that upset us.

The constructive emotions are curiosity, joy, pleasure, love. Of these, it is suggested that the capacity to experience curiosity, joy, pleasure and love is innate, but the means of expression are learned.

The destructive emotions are fear, worry, anxiety, anger, jealousy and sorrow. Of these, fear is inborn. We see evidence of this at birth in the startle reflex, before the child has had experience to

A *predominance of good experience*

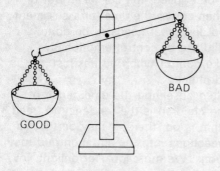

problem solving ability
frustration tolerance
sympathy/understanding/affection
general tolerance
happiness — shared and enjoyed
sadness overcome
sense of value/self confidence

B *excess of good experience — overprotection*

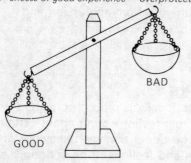

inability to cope with adversity
self interest
inability to understand other
    people's problems
low frustration tolerance

C *excess of bad experience*

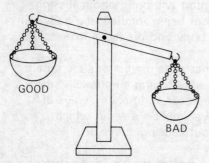

difficulty in making
    affectionate relationships
inability to solve problems
apathy and/or aggression
introversion
physical and mental ill health

Fig 9.1   balance of emotional experience

learn fear. Anger could also be considered innate since we are
left in no doubt as to the emotions of a hungry or neglected
baby. He expresses his anger in lengthy bouts of crying.

Perhaps anxiety, worry, jealousy and sorrow are learned. The
implication is that the child learns to imitate certain emotions.
Given love most children will respond in an affectionate way. If a
child sees an adult express fear e.g. in a thunderstorm, he too
will become fearful of thunder.

Every child is subjected to both constructive and destructive experiences. These are necessary for his development in order that he may mature into a spontaneously responsive adult who is capable of sharing good emotions and understanding bad ones. It is, however, desirable that good emotional experience should be dominant for healthy development. Good and bad emotional experience must be balanced so that the child will be a happy child, but also one who has a degree of frustration tolerance and the ability to control unpleasant feelings.

A child deprived of love may become an adult unable to make satisfactory loving relationships. The child protected from sorrow will lack understanding. The child prevented from exploiting curiosity will lack the spirit of exploration and adventure.

As in every other sphere of development, so in emotional development, the child needs the opportunity to practise his skills and learn from his success or failure.

LEARNING EMOTIONAL CONTROL

The various ways in which we express emotion are conditioned to a large extent by the society in which we live. The British are famous for their 'stiff upper lip'. We have acquired a reputation, largely borne out of the Victorian era, for gritting our teeth and not expressing emotion in a physical way or in a way that will embarrass those around us. This may present a veneer of outward calm, but the suppression of violent emotions leads to frustration and stress. In the long term it would perhaps be healthier to 'let off steam' and channel such violent energy into constructive use.

On the whole it is accepted that laughter and physical expressions of pleasure are acceptable. Crying, on the other hand, is acceptable in young children, but in a supposedly mature adult is often considered a sign of emotional immaturity. In other cultures, this may not be the case. Crying is considered a socially acceptable manner in which to express extreme sorrow or joy.

It is not then sensible or practical to consider emotional development unless we first consider the norms of the society in which the child is growing up. This presents great difficulty for ethnic minorities in any country where social restraints operate differently in the **culture** into which the child is born and the environment in which he will grow up. It is just this type of conflict which causes frustration and intolerance between immigrants and the indigenous population.

DEVELOPMENTAL TRENDS

Some emotions are contagious. This implies that the child imitates certain emotional reactions. Even very young babies will whimper when they hear another baby crying. A toddler will become distressed at hearing his younger brother or sister crying even if he is too young to appreciate the cause of the distress. He too will become composed once the baby is comforted. With increasing maturity, this occurs less often, but even adults can be affected by a feeling of emotion stirring around them, particularly in a crowd situation.

Due to the short concentration span in young children, emotional outbursts tend to be immediate, violent and brief. Small children seldom bear grudges or sulk. Bouts of sulking should be tolerated but not necessarily encouraged since this is a sign of stress going inwards and does not really allow the child to solve his problem. The caring adult will observe this trend and by example and encouragement show the child a more useful way in which to channel his aggression. Because his intellectual development is immature and his experience limited, the young child may not understand the cause of his violent feelings, and he needs to express himself in a physical way to release the pent-up feelings. As his language skill and understanding develop, suitable words and gestures will replace the total body response.

Children's emotional responses vary from child to child, according to maturity and experience, but there is little doubt that children's emotions can be detected by their behaviour. This is not necessarily the case in the adult, who has been conditioned by society to hide or control his feelings. Perhaps adults could learn from the children that an outburst need not be feared or cause embarrassment and may bring quicker relief from inner stress. Too often it is felt that emotionality brings punishment or rejection and only the most secure adult will permit himself this luxury in the knowledge that his friends will still accept him.

Emotion is a driving force — one to be reckoned with and used to good purpose. Feelings may not change in intensity as one grows older, but the response to those feelings is often modified in the light of knowledge and experience and with the development of problem solving ability.

It has been suggested that children pass through periods of increased emotional behaviour. The greatest effects of this heightened emotion are seen in children demonstrating exaggerated 'destructive' emotions e.g. fear, worry, anger. Possibly the emotions appear exaggerated because the adult too is experiencing an emotional conflict with the child, who may not be conforming at that stage in his development. Whatever the origin, uncontrolled emotions can, if prolonged, cause physical upset in a young child, and the caring adult should be aware that this is developing and intervene to prevent a child from reaching a situation with which he cannot cope. Prolonged crying, due to anger, can upset the young baby by interfering with the digestive mechanisms. In crying, he will swallow much air and then be subjected to the discomfort of wind which might lead to vomiting. His heart and respiration rates will rise. Add to this the degree of energy expended in total body activity and a very tired baby will result.

The over excited 4 year old may vomit, become temporarily incontinent or fail to drop off to sleep at night. Increased emotional responses are often due to adjustments to a period of rapid growth or a new situation and should therefore be temporary, but if the child is constantly surrounded by poor examples in the family e.g. rejection or excessive tension he may develop a pattern of over reacting himself.

In order to provide a child with the skills with which to use his emotions to good effect, we must care for his physical wellbeing, help him to develop a sense of humour, accept that 'a good cry' has a therapeutic value and listen when he wants to talk out his difficulties. A respect for his point of view when his needs conflict with ours is an attribute that will help to avoid confrontations. At all times, he needs a close, affectionate relationship with the important adults in his life — adults who will go on loving him when he is at his least lovable.

DEVELOPMENT OF EMOTIONAL STABILITY
A young child's emotional stability hinges largely on whether he is accepted or rejected by his most important adults. The child who develops within an 'accepting' environment where there is consistency of temperament and mutual joy in family life will bounce back in the face of adversity. On the other hand, the rejected child is likely to suffer physical and emotional traumas.

Acceptance
To deliver a baby to her new mother, place it in her arms and say, 'Now love this baby' is unrealistic. Love must grow, fostered by continuity of the relationship and the reward of response from the child. To expect 'acceptance' of a healthy child is realistic. The mother who suffers disappointment of one kind or another at the birth of the child e.g. a handicapped or ill baby, may need sensitive care and tolerant help if she is going to 'accept' her child.

'Emotional bonding' is the term applied to this early acceptance of a baby by its mother. In my view, the baby is the receiver, the mother the giver, at this early stage. So important is this attachment that it is actively fostered by paediatricians, obstetricians, health visitors, midwives and general practitioners.

Mothers are encouraged to fondle, talk to and suckle their babies as soon as possible after delivery. For those unfortunate mothers whose babies require special care or incubator therapy in the early weeks of life and are deprived of this closeness, facilities are made for them to observe and touch their babies, feed them when the child is well enough. At the very least the mother is encouraged to express her milk for her baby. This is then fed via tube or bottle.

Fig 9.2   '... "emotional bonding" ... the baby is the receiver, the mother the giver ...'

Little is said of emotional bonding between father and child. Tacit recognition is given to the fact that it occurs but it doesn't receive the attention it deserves. Perhaps the greatest step in the right direction is the recent encouragement given to the father to take part in the ante-natal preparation of his partner and to share with her the experience of childbirth.

Love implies many aspects of care and is the basis of a child's healthy development. Love, as it grows, must be given as of right, not as reward. Each parent's expression of love varies according to personality, but is often a reflection of his/her own experience in childhood. Most adults have feelings of protection towards babies and young children. From these protective feelings grows the love that permits freedom of movement and expression; the love that allows the child to experience good and bad emotions within a safe and loving environment; the love that encourages curiosity, stimulates learning; the love that provides a moral framework and guides the development of accepted standards.

Rejection

Rejection of a child by its mother and father is a situation that many of us would be shocked by. As with many things, it is a question of degree. To some extent rejection occurs in all parent/child relationships at some time, however superficial or temporary.

Every mother who has a baby makes a sacrifice of some kind. It may be a sacrifice of time, leisure, money, career.

Sadly, rejection of children seems to be a facet of life in this and other cultures. Not a new problem, but one which has come into the limelight in recent years and has become the subject of great inquiry, discussion and legislation. To understand rejection we need to examine some of its causes.

Causes of rejection – relating to parents
1 *illegitimacy or a pregnancy that is the cause of marriage*
2 *abandonment of a career by the mother or father*
3 *disharmony* – the child being the only tie between the parents
4 *mixed partnerships* – where the differences of race, religion, social classes etc, put strain upon the relationship.

Several factors contributing to rejection could exist within the emotional make-up of the parents, especially when either or both is emotionally immature or where the parents themselves experienced rejection as children.

Where the child fails to meet the expectations of the parents, factors relating to the child can cause rejection. These include:

1 a child of the 'wrong' sex
2 handicap – mental or physical
3 an adopted child
4 an ill child.

A mother who experiences physical harm during the pregnancy or delivery may blame her child for this discomfort.

Rejection can take many forms, the most obvious of which is neglect, ill treatment, abuse. The subtlety lies in whether or not the child feels neglected. Occasionally a child may imagine rejection where none exists e.g. at the birth of another child, when he goes to school or when he or his mother has to be

Fig 9.3   '... a child may imagine rejection where none exists ...'

hospitalised. These 3 are all situations of separation of varying degrees, and may be viewed as rejection by a small child.

We all experience rejection at some time and must therefore learn to cope with it. Rejection only becomes harmful when it is physically damaging, extreme or prolonged. An inherently strong child may overcome such abuse and achieve stability through learning, experience or a changed environment that tempers the imbalance. Throughout life the adult who was damaged emotionally in childhood remains vulnerable to stress.

Pattern of emotional response caused by separation from the mother

The study of this behaviour is often made of children who are admitted to hospital. Perhaps this is biased, because admission to hospital is a rather special situation, almost always accompanied by discomfort or fear borne out of pain, or a strange environment. However, as a result of such research much has been achieved to alleviate this distress by *not* separating mother and child when they are especially vulnerable, and it is the rule to admit them together whenever possible. However, the following pattern of behaviour, I would suggest, is seen at *any* time when a young child is separated from his mother or caring adult. The time it lasts and the degree of its effect vary according to the circumstances, the length of the separation and the stage of development reached by the child.

Initially, the child protests. He cries, he shouts, he thumps, he bangs, then he goes very quiet, he sulks, he sobs. He indulges in some kind of self comfort like thumb sucking or fondling his genitals. (A really distressed child may sit for some time rocking to and fro or resort to banging his head against a hard surface.)

At this stage in his distress, re-appearance of the mother often results in the child rejecting her. If she is tolerant, patient and approaches the child with understanding, gradually the child begins to respond to her again.

To a lesser degree, this behaviour will be observed in the baby approaching 1 year of age whose mother leaves the room in which he is playing to go about her housework. It may be seen in the young child experiencing his 1st day away from his mother in the care of a friend, or at school. The mother of a child who has recently started school may remark that the child is a horror when

Fig 9.4   self comfort

she collects him at home time, although the teacher may report that once he settled he was 'good as gold'. This is the child saying to his mother, 'You left me all day!' Gradually, on the way home, they become friends again.

Behaviour of this kind at the end of a busy day is often exacerbated by hunger and a low blood sugar. A sweet or ice cream on the way home, or a snack when he arrives, will help the child regain his composure.

Human beings function best in groups. Most people like to be an accepted member of the group. Rejection, however slight, hurts at any age, even in adult life — the difference being that the adult is experienced and his/her responses have been modified by learning and the maturing process. Also an adult does not suffer the bewilderment that increases the distress of the young child.

To be accepting, to be affectionate should be the aim of all those who care for young children. The sense of security so gained will help the child to realise that what he does is important; he has value. His confidence builds and shows good effect on all aspects of his development. He will thrive physically, learn more readily and integrate socially with a minimum of setbacks.

10
Social development

Social development means development of the ability to behave in accordance with the expectations of society. It follows, therefore, that social development is entirely dependent upon the environment, culture, religious belief of the family into which the child is born. One very important facet of social development is communication. Language development and non-verbal communication are of equal importance. Three processes are involved:

1 Proper behaviour
What is proper behaviour? Every social group has its code of acceptable behaviour. Gradually every child must learn what that code is and model his own behaviour on the example set by those around him. (Reflect upon the problems of the child of immigrant parents who is trying to identify with 2 groups simultaneously.) Everyday codes of behaviour include the wearing of appropriate clothing, eating in a polite manner using the customary utensils and cutlery, and using correct forms of communication.

The sooner a child can use language fluently the sooner he can express himself clearly and there is less likelihood that his meaning will be misunderstood. Non-verbal communication, whilst giving emphasis to aspects of speech, may be misinterpreted. One of the baby's earliest forms of non-verbal communication is crying. The meaning of crying is very often arrived at by a process of elimination. He has just been fed so he is unlikely to be hungry, but he might have wind. He has just been washed and his napkin has been changed, so he cannot be soiled and uncomfortable. In this way a mother learns to interpret the cry.

Is a baby born knowing that a smile indicates pleasure? It is very unlikely. However, since smiles evoke a pleasant response and are usually associated with the nicer things in life, he imitates the smile. He learns quickly that poking, prodding, pinching are acceptable if they form part of a romp, but bring disapproval at other times. He is praised when he manages to put food in his mouth instead of down his jersey, so that must be the right way.

Apart from the everyday codes of behaviour, there are occasions in our lives when a special form of behaviour is the accepted norm e.g. marriage or death in the circle of family or friends. Not only do these occasions require a special behaviour, they demand a code of language and dress and form part of our culture.

In our society these codes have become less restraining over the years. Using death as an example, at one time in Britain, the family of the deceased celebrated a prescribed period of mourning during which time selected callers would be received, dress would be sombre and there was a set of rules for the behaviour of the bereaved. With the passing of time, many of these customs have been abandoned, but not replaced by any other recognised form of behaviour. This void may account for the embarrassment surrounding death. Do we or do we not talk about it? What should we wear for the funeral? Should we have a 'ham tea and a good send off' or would a polite glass of sherry suffice?

Slowly but surely children are taught the social skills which will help them to make relationships and live happily in the community.

2 Playing approved social roles

A social role is a pattern of behaviour expected of a person in given circumstances. One person is called upon to play many roles during a lifetime. We move through childhood and adolescence to adult life; from the family through school to the wider world of work, marriage, parenthood and finally old age. Many of these changes take place through growth and maturation, other changes take place by the roles we adopt, some of which are determined by society, others we choose for ourselves.

As a practical example, let us examine the situation of the young working wife, who is also a mother and teacher. At different times she must be wife to her husband, mother to her children, teacher to her pupils, daughter to her own mother etc, etc. In most cases we can change fairly easily from one role to the other as the situation demands, but difficulties arise when we are expected to fulfil 2 roles at once and there is conflict of loyalties, perhaps.

For the young child, learning to 'wear different hats at different times' can be difficult, particularly when roles are in conflict. Very early on in life a young child may have established his role as 'child', and then another child comes along. Over a period of years, maybe, he has to learn the role of being a brother whilst still being the child of his parents. Very often this conflict of roles leads to sibling rivalries and upset.

To complicate the issue further, grandmother and grandfather expect the child to be a grandchild too and here an entirely different set of rules apply – rules which may cause disagreement between grandmother and mother. How difficult it is learning to be social!

Well defined sex roles still exist in some cultures and in some families who live in a society which generally has abandoned this clear distinction. Obviously, adult men and women will never be able to fulfil exactly the same role by virtue of their respective genetic masculinity or femininity. However, in some societies the roles intermingle more now than they have done in the past. In the western cultures a small boy may still be told, 'Little boys don't wear skirts', even if he is merely playing at dressing-up – an early lesson in what is proper dress for a boy. At one time, little boys were discouraged from playing with dolls, sewing and cooking; little girls did not wear trousers, play at cowboys and Indians or do woodwork. Now the emphasis is on widening a child's experience in every possible direction. Most boys and girls now have the opportunity to explore the male and female world as far as biological development permits. As a result we have some very capable male midwives and nurses, and some female engineers who can compete on equal terms with any male counterpart. One very positive and beneficial result of role adaptation is that many men take a more active part in family matters generally and the care of their young families particularly. Many women combine childbearing with a professional career. In some families role reversal exists: the woman bears the child, subsequently returns to work after maternity leave and the man gives up his job to stay at home and complete the household duties.

3 Development of social attitudes

A sense of belonging to and being accepted in a group; human beings are gregarious by nature but being a group member requires knowledge, co-operation, control of one's impulses.

Controlling one's impulses comes with maturity. For the child much of his social development centres around learning how to control aggression and cope with frustration. He learns to use the energy generated by aggression for a constructive purpose.

Co-operation, a sense of which develops early in childhood, will result if the child's efforts at it are accepted and rewarding. Learning these lessons is difficult. To learn them well he must develop imagination, sympathy and possibly even try to understand what it would be like to be someone else.

To sum up, adequate social development means that the child behaves and speaks in such a way that he will fit into the social group with which he wishes to be identified and will be accepted by the group as a member. He will, in fact, learn the 'rules of the club'.

LEARNING TO BE SOCIAL
It is fair to say that the home is the seat of learning for the development of social skills and the desire to make relationships with other people. The deep relationships which exist between a child and his family give him the confidence to venture into relationships with outsiders and it is the family that makes the first introductions and creates the opportunities for the child.

A nursery school or playgroup, where there is direction and guidance in making social contacts successfully, provides a child with excellent safe opportunities for learning to be social with other adults and children. By trial and error a child will learn some of the behaviour patterns necessary for good social adjustments. He may learn to get along with others by imitation. He observes what others do and then practises the effect by pretending to be that person. A boy, for example, learns to be a father by observing his own father; he observes what being a husband means. As there is very little formal training for these most vital roles, it is therefore very important that the child has a good example to copy and the opportunity to do so.

Occasionally, it is necessary for the adult to actively teach the child social behaviour. Simple examples are saying 'please' and 'thank you'. Properly managed toilet practice is a way in which we teach children social behaviour. Of paramount importance is that the adult shows to the child the respect he is due and by example instils habits of politeness. If a child is successful in his early attempts at social behaviour he is likely to adopt that form of conduct. The important thing is that he develops a will to please and a desire for acceptance.

The unfortunate child who is deprived of social guidance may develop anti-social traits. Once established, these cause considerable emotional and social damage and may bring the child into conflict with the law.

DEVELOPMENTAL TRENDS
The first social responses are to a face, usually the face of an important adult. Within 6–8 weeks he will smile in response to a smile, he will turn his eyes when he hears a human voice. He

Fig 10.1 'The first social responses are to a face ...'

practises his new skill alone, but is encouraged and becomes excited in the presence of receptive members of his family. He shows his pleasure by total body movement.

During the 3rd month, babies begin to show more specific responses to social situations. Some will stop crying when they are talked to or cuddled. Most babies at this time recognise their important people and begin to discriminate between who is family and who is not. Already he is showing a desire to belong. He hates to be excluded from the group and is distressed if left alone for too long. Physical play, at mother distance, forms an important part of his day. He loves to be bounced on a knee, test the weight of his body by standing on a lap. Pat-a-cake and peek-a-boo games evoke chuckles and delighted gurgles. He shows interest in his own reflection in a mirror. His social advances are physical and exploratory. He pulls at hair, spectacles, noses. In the company of other babies he explores them too, by grasping, poking, prodding, pulling at clothes and features. Pets, too, will experience the vigour with which he pursues them and makes social advances.

Approaching 1 year old he responds to verbal directions. He refrains from doing something in response to 'no'. He is suspicious

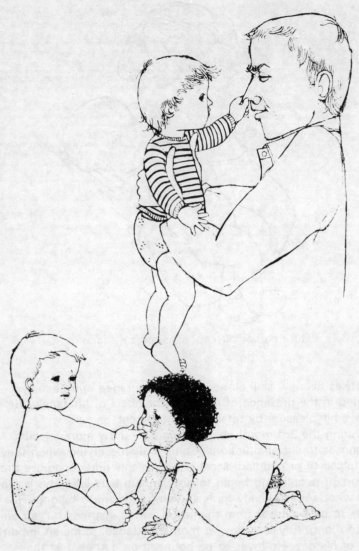

Fig 10.2 'His social advances are physical and exploratory.'

of strangers but loving with his favourite toys and people. As his language develops, he shows an increasing interest in others and a strong desire to be with them and imitate them. He will play happily alongside other children but has not yet developed the desire to be part of their play. Human beings are gregarious animals, preferring the company of others, but the ability to enter into a social relationship takes maturity and rewarding practice.

This will develop after he has had time to observe, imitate and make varied attempts to co-operate. So, in a short period of time, the baby has changed from a passive member of the group to an active participant who is showing signs of accepting some social guidance and taking some responsibility for his own care. He learns that in our society it is the norm to wear clothes and he can now assist with pushing an arm into a coat or removing shoes and socks. Feeding is performed using a spoon and fork as well as fingers and he sits on a chair at a table to do it. Excretion requires the use of a pot or lavatory, cleansing and handwashing – all things that are part of our culture and have previously been done for him by the caring adult.

These are all steps along the way to being socialised – necessary steps if he is to become an accepted member of a community. He is doing very well in so short a time; however, much has still to be learned about making relationships. By about the age of 4 years children begin to show signs of playing together. At this stage they are naturally still very self centred. Their conversation reveals a predominance of 'me' and 'my' so it is not surprising that the friendships of this age are born out of convenient co-operation i.e. they will co-operate when it is in their own best interests to do so. It will be some time before the more mature friendship based on giving rather than taking is formed. From time to time, when he is unsure of himself, he will revert to a less mature form of behaviour. Don't we all! Even the 'mature' adult will behave in an immature way in an insecure situation.

So much to learn – how do we help him? By providing a good example; by providing satisfactory play experience and the opportunities to practise new social skills; and last but not least, by encouraging the acquisition of skills and making the performance of them rewarding. We can engage him in conversation, listen to his explanations and stories, and help him to use the skill of language to express himself.

SCHOOL – A SOCIALISING INFLUENCE

With entry to school, be it nursery or first school, a child is exposed to different socialising agents. At an egocentric stage in his development he must learn group awareness. He now has to share the important adult, the teacher or nursery nurse, with many other children all making similar demands on the adult's time and patience. School takes up a large proportion of the child's waking hours and will therefore have special significance as the second most important influence on his social behaviour after the family group.

School presents the child with the real world. A world of contrived and naturally evolving groups each with its own quite different set of rules. He will be assigned to a class but must now choose his friends from a large number of strangers. Classroom rules will be different from playground rules. If he stays for school lunch he will be supervised by catering service staff. Not only are they different people from teacher in that they perform different functions for him, their expectation of him is different.

School is competitive. School has an unfamiliar hierarchy of authority. Adults in school may use a different type of language from what he has learnt at home. He is unlikely to experience the freedom at school that he has enjoyed at home. Amazingly, most children make the necessary adaptations remarkably quickly. So efficiently in fact that the mother of a child in his 1st year at school will often say, 'He's no longer mine'. She is recognising that, for the moment at least, school is influencing her child as much as she is. She has to learn to share her child with his teacher.

School entry also marks the beginning of **peer group** influence. At his peril the child will foster acceptance by the teacher and not peer group acceptance. He seeks approval by the group, but friendship from a few. Friendships become very staunch at this stage of a child's life. Separation from the 'best friend' for even a short while can upset a child considerably. Satisfactory adjustment to school is based largely on previous experience, but also on his attitude to going to school and the care he receives there. Going to school is seen as a mark of being grown-up and most children look forward to school.

Although learning to be social continues throughout life, early childhood experience is of special importance. Impressions and attitudes formed in the first 5–7 years of life leave a profound imprint on the personality and behaviour as an adult. A secure child who has developed confidence in his social relationships is likely to grow into a friendly, affectionate adult who enjoys new experiences and accepts adversity as a challenge. He will bring his abilities, energies and problem solving techniques to the demands of life.

DEVELOPING A SENSE OF MORALS
Our word moral is derived from a Latin word, meaning manner or custom.

Without denying the presence of inherited personality traits it is possible to describe the newborn baby as amoral. The morals or values that we come to adopt are largely influenced by environmental factors. Specifically, the culture or religion into which a child is born will have evolved a system of rules which are designed to protect that community. Within the community, each family will have certain 'rules' that control the behaviour of the members of that family.

Society writes down its rules. The family has no need to because attitudes and feelings permeate the day's happenings almost unnoticed, but the growing child will internalise them and adopt many of them as his own. By watching adults and imitating their behaviour and manner of speaking, the developing child tests out the success of his behaviour. The reactions of others to him will determine whether or not he has behaved in a socially acceptable way, spoken without causing offence.

In his social advances to other children, he will quickly learn what is 'fair', what is 'unfair'. He will hopefully learn that honesty is expected and untruths bring disapproval. He will develop a concept of kindness and unkindness. He will soon learn that adults are more likely to make allowances for his lapses and his peers will not. The adult will often explain why he failed and show him a more successful way to achieve his ends. In his relationships with other children who themselves are learning the 'rules of the game', he may experience violence in response to his behaviour and may be totally bewildered by the apparent injustice. As well as setting a good example, the adult must be near at hand to rescue him when he is out of his depth.

Conversation and stories help to reinforce the developing sense of what is 'right' and what is 'wrong'. As well as learning the general principles, he must learn that what constitutes right behaviour in one situation can be wrong behaviour in another. We must guide him, protect him from exposure to morally harmful experiences and buffer his disappointments.

Development from the amoral baby to a child with a reasonably well developed sense of what is right and what is wrong takes about 5 years. After that, having developed an awareness of the black and the white extremes he will learn that morality has many grey areas that require experience and knowledge for him to make up his own mind on certain issues.

This is a complicated world. To 'lie' is wrong but a 'fib' or 'white lie' is often acceptable. To steal is wrong. Is it wrong to pocket the small coin he finds in the street? It is wrong to hurt other people. Is his mother justified in smacking him? In order to understand 'stealing' a child must have a concept of 'mine' and 'yours'. To lie, the child must first distinguish between reality and fantasy. He will not understand why physical violence hurts unless he himself has been hurt. He also needs imagination to appreciate why, when inflicting violence, the other person experiences discomfort and stress.

The adult's golden rule is, 'Be as consistent as humanly possible.' Make a minimum of rules for children and then only when the rule is designed to protect him or other people and their property. Once the rule is made it must be obeyed. If something is wrong today, it is wrong tomorrow and every other day.

Do not face a young child with choices. He has not the experience to enable him to take a reasonable decision. Boundaries need to be drawn for young children. They derive security from being contained. The time for discussion, argument and investigation of the 'grey areas' comes later, much later, when language, reasoning and understanding have developed and the child is capable of accepting a compromise.

THE FAMILY

The concept of the family varies according to one's country of origin, faith and experience. Generally, we consider the family as comprising parents and children living together in one household. However, there are many variations on this theme: a theme which is constantly changing as patterns in society change and ideas become more liberal. In spite of the differences encountered in family groupings, certain functions are common to all.

The primary function of a family is continuation of the species, namely childbearing and childrearing. By providing a home and consistent affection parents are contributing to the satisfactory physical, emotional and social development of the child. Given a stimulating home and interested parents, satisfactory intellectual development should follow.

The importance of growing up in secure surroundings with caring adults cannot be stressed too much since the family is providing the next generation of adults who will then go on to reproduce and influence the lives of yet another generation. Children learn parental roles largely from what they themselves experience within the family, so it is important that the example set is a good one. A facet of security is a feeling of belonging. The pattern of loyalty, unity and group identity that a child experiences at home is a sound foundation upon which to build his own life.

The family is a safe place in which to 'lick one's wounds' – a retreat providing freedom of expression which is received with sympathy and total acceptance. The child who is unable to solve his problems within the family may develop destructive ways of releasing his inner tensions.

It is preferable that a family supports itself financially. In the past it has been the role of the man to provide and the woman to manage, but increasingly, women with or without children are continuing to work or returning to work in order to supplement the income or satisfy their own personal needs. Many marriages have become a partnership of equals. The dominant male is less dominating. More women are demanding the right to choose between homemaking and childrearing and the continuance of a career. In the long term it is the personality of the individual which determines the success of the chosen way of life.

A significant change in family structure has arisen due to an increasing mobility within the community generally. In some communities we still find the nuclear family (parents and children) living within easy access of the extended family (grandparents, aunts, uncles etc). The situation still exists where the young woman who marries lives a few streets away from her mother and father, in-laws, brothers and sisters. We also find large numbers of young couples moving away from home in search of job opportunities or training facilities, cheaper housing or numerous other personal factors. Either way, the extended family still has a vital role to play in providing a source of comfort, advice and security. If only in times of stress, support by the extended family is invaluable. Problem solving and the sharing of adversity help to reinforce relationships already existing.

If we pass beyond the boundary of 'family', to the community, each family grouped with others helps to comprise that community. The passing on of traditions, codes of behaviour and community awareness is an integral part of day to day living within a home. The aware family will take an active part in and help to stabilise the community in which it lives, by partaking in communal activities whether social, recreational, political or at worship. Satisfactory relationships built up in the family will provide the child with the self assurance and confidence he needs to assume responsibilities within the community as he matures.

The degree of success with which the family functions will affect, for good or ill, the health of the immediate community and ultimately the wider society. By its constructive contribution, both moral and financial, the family is helping to ensure the wellbeing and satisfactory progress of that society.

So far, we have considered only the family as it exists in this and other western countries. There are people who have developed alternative systems of childrearing e.g. the **kibbutzim** in Israel. Elsewhere we find more than one wife sharing a husband who is likely to be the father of many, many children. Another system is the communal system of family life. This may mean a group of nuclear families living together and sharing the 'family' responsibilities in a communal way. Alternatively, it may mean a variety of adults caring for a variety of children from a variety of sexual unions. This will result in a degree of in-breeding and some complicated family systems may emerge.

For many and varied reasons, numerous families have only one parent. In terms of the children, this need not be the disadvantage it appears at first. Possibly the greatest obstacle to be overcome is the demands made upon that one parent and the lack of support he or she suffers by being alone.

Inadequate finance may prove the greatest hazard to family harmony, since the single parent may only manage part time employment if he/she is to devote the necessary time to the children and home. Conversely, full time employment could result in the emotional and social needs of the child being neglected by a parent who is too tired to cope. This is a 'cleft stick' dilemma which can only be solved by the particular family in its own personal way.

THE FAMILY AS A DEVELOPING UNIT
All too frequently we consider the family as a static unit. Rather, the family, by nature of the individuals comprising it, is changing, constantly maturing as the members mature. Roles within the family change, not only because the years of childhood are short, but because the parents themselves are maturing at a different level. The family must be considered as a growing organism, passing through its own sequence of development. A pattern which is influenced by the ages of both parents and children and the desired quality of family life.

At the beginning, we have the couple without children. Each of the pair fulfilling the role demanded of a one-to-one relationship which increases in depth and intensity as the couple become more experienced at being together. As the couple arrive at the physical and psychological stage of readiness for childrearing, decisions will be made concerning the number and spacing of children.

With the birth of the first child, stage 2 is entered and with this event changes in role take place. A new stage in the sequence of family development is reached. The child must conform to the pattern of life established by the parents and the parents take on the roles and responsibilities of childrearing. Due to the physical demands of feeding and general care, it is possible that the mother

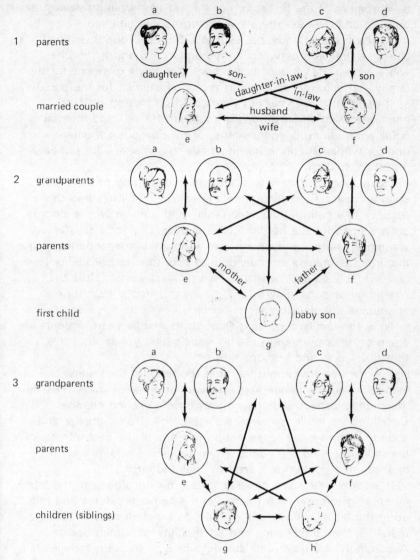

Fig 10.3   role changes in a developing family

figure will assume greatest importance for the child at this time. Gradually, other important adults increasingly come to fill part of the child's life as his awareness and perception develops.

During the pre-school years of the first child's life, chances are that a 2nd child will be born into this unit of 3 and the relationships hitherto formed will expand to accommodate the needs of a 4th member — a member who will make added demands upon the parents, but who will significantly affect the development of the firstborn. For the 1st time sibling rivalries may be seen and may exaggerate with subsequent children.

As the first child adventures into school life, opportunities for a closer relationship between the younger child and his mother will emerge. The influence of school is a new experience for the family. School entry requires as much adjustment for the parents as it does for the 5 year old who could be making his first encounter with larger groups of children. He will find the caring adult with whom he spends most of his day is not a parent and one for whose attention he may have to compete with possibly 30 other children.

Ultimately, the family will become a 'launching pad' for older children nearing complete independence but still needing the security of a caring, interested family and a home whose door is always open for the frequent returns necessary for a satisfactory weaning period — a weaning from supported independence to the maturity that allows an individual to take total responsibility for his own actions and carve his own niche in society. It is the overriding responsibility of any parent or parental substitute to encourage this development.

Now the family is passing through its middle years. Parents are again on their own and possibly anticipating yet another role, that of in-laws and grandparents.

It is hardly surprising, then, that the tasks of the family members and the family as a unit vary at different stages. Possibly the saddest aspect is that we never have a second chance. Decisions are made, patterns are established, roles emerge and change and, in most cases, action taken is in the best interest of the individual and the whole. However, success is difficult to measure and is often achieved by trial and error.

It is only when we consider this growing organism, the family, attempting to cope with internal and external pressures and reflect upon the tasks it must fulfil in order to function happily that we marvel at the competence and adaptability of human beings. Accordingly, we gain understanding of why so many families fail.

11
The brain and intellectual development

The human brain is the largest and most complex brain in the animal kingdom. The adult brain weighs approximately 1.36 kilogrammes and brain growth proceeds more rapidly during foetal life and infancy than in any other body structure. At birth, about 25% of total growth has taken place, at 5 years approximately 90% and the remaining growth proceeds more slowly to arrive at total brain growth by adult life.

THE BRAIN
The brain is contained within the skull and protected by the membranes which cover it and cerebro-spinal fluid which acts as a shock absorber. The dura mater lines the skull and is the toughest of the 3 membranes. The arachnoid membrane contains the cerebro-spinal fluid and the pia mater, a delicate membrane, covers the substance of the brain and spinal cord and supports a network of fine blood vessels. It is these 3 membranes, collectively known as the meninges, that are inflamed in the condition of meningitis ('itis' – inflammation; 'mening' – the meninges).

The brain and the spinal cord make up the central nervous system. The spinal cord is the 'trunk road' along which impulses travel. The brain controls and co-ordinates nervous activity and consists of the following structures:

The cerebrum
This forms the greatest part of the brain. It consists of 2 linked hemispheres, the outer coat of which is termed the cortex. This vital part of the brain receives sensory impulses, sends out impulses that bring about the desired motor response and governs the activities of the rest of the brain. The cerebral cortex contains about 90% of the nerve cells.

Beneath the cerebral cortex lie large uncharted areas of the cerebral hemispheres that are probably concerned with the mental processes of intelligence, memory, judgement, imagination, and creative thought and conscious thought.

The cerebellum
This lies at the back and below the cerebrum. It also has 2 hemispheres and is highly complex in function. John Brierley, in his book *The Growing Brain*,* describes this structure as 'the automatic pilot'. It co-ordinates body movement, making precise movement possible, and maintains balance.

The pons
This is continuous with the medulla oblongata. As its name implies, the pons forms a bridge which links the two halves of the cerebellum. It contains some vital involuntary centres e.g. part of the respiratory centre.

The medulla oblongata
The medulla is continuous with the spinal cord. It contains the involuntary centres which control heart beat, respiration, body temperature, digestion. It also houses the area in which the motor fibres cross over. This means that the right side of the brain controls the left side of the body and vice versa.

Nervous tissue
This is made up of cells called neurones. It is useful to compare nerves and the conduction of impulses with electric wires and the conduction of electricity. If we cut across a multi-core flex we would see a number of wires, each well insulated to ensure that the electric current does not short out, but is conducted safely from one place to another. Many nerves are constructed in a similar way. Individual nerve fibres are 'insulated' by a substance known as myelin. Many nerve fibres have not developed this insulating sheath before birth and some smaller ones never do. This process, known as myelination, continues throughout the period of brain growth. The myelin sheath not only insulates, but also speeds up the conduction of impulses.

Some sensory nerves myelinate before the motor nerves. It is no accident that the child's senses are so well developed at birth. The senses are conveyors of information and often have a protective function. It is important to remember this, and to provide the young child with all types of sensory experience from the beginning of life. Most adults accept that a small baby has an inherent desire to be active and much encouragement is given to help him adjust his posture and eventually walk. As well as this, we

* *The Growing Brain: Childhood's Crucial Years*, by John Brierley. National Foundation for Educational Research, 1976.

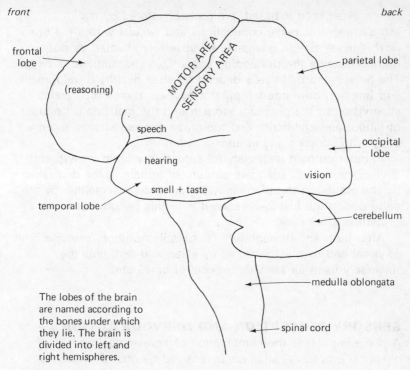

front

back

frontal lobe

(reasoning)

MOTOR AREA

SENSORY AREA

parietal lobe

speech

occipital lobe

hearing

vision

smell + taste

temporal lobe

cerebellum

The lobes of the brain
are named according to
the bones under which
they lie. The brain is
divided into left and
right hemispheres.

medulla oblongata

spinal cord

Fig 11.1   left side view of the brain

should remember that he has the mechanisms for sensory
experience and we should surround him with sights, sounds, tastes,
smells and particularly tactile experience.

During foetal life, the child is constantly surrounded by the
womb, which can be described as total touch experience. At birth,
this physical bond is broken and we must continue the cradling,
nursing and body contact as we wean him towards independence.

This pattern of growth, myelination of sensory nerves before
growth and myelination of motor nerves, is necessary if the motor
system is to function in response to a sensory stimulus. The baby,
stimulated by the sight of his favourite adult's face looking over
his cot, will extend both arms in anticipation of being lifted. (See
Figure 11.2) As stated previously, this voluntary movement cannot
take place until the nervous system has matured sufficiently to
control the muscle action.

Growth, myelination and the branching of nerves to create a
mature nervous system are processes about which we still have
much to learn. They appear to be processes that progress with
brain development and are improved by exercise of the brain
functions; that is, brain function improves with use. Memories, on

123

which experience is based, are probably stored by the establishment of nerve connections and circuits within the brain.

This development is apparently adversely affected by poor nutrition during the developing years. One vital nutrient is oxygen. The nerves and brain cells depend for their healthy development and function on a good supply of oxygen. Hence the careful supervision of the pregnant woman and the meticulous conduct of labour and childbirth, and the grave concern shown about a baby who shows signs of anoxia at birth.

Another nutrient necessary for satisfactory brain growth and development is an adequate amount of protein in the diet taken by the mother in the pregnancy period and subsequently by the child during the first 2–3 years. It is in this period that brain growth is at its peak.

After birth and throughout life, suitable nutrition, exercise both physical and mental, balanced by sleep and rest, plus the necessary fresh air are vital aspects of brain care.

SENSORY PERCEPTION AND NERVOUS ACTION

A nerve impulse is the combination of an electrical and a chemical process. A stimulus is received by one of the sense organs and transmitted to the brain which interprets this message as one or more of the distinct types of sensations: touch or pressure, temperature, pain, taste, smell, hearing, balance, sight. Particular regions of the brain deal only with particular regions of the body, therefore interpretation of the position and type of sensation experienced is possible.

Nerve branching and the nervous pathways that develop in the brain cause reasoning, recall and memory, emotional feelings such as joy and sorrow etc; the motor neurones convey impulses to the muscles for the appropriate action to be taken.

The simplest, yet one of the most important and efficient forms of nerve action is the reflex action. This is an involuntary action following immediately upon a specific stimulus and is directly relevant to that stimulus. The time elapsing between stimulation and response is minimal. Many reflex actions are protective: for example, if we touch something very hot, the hand is withdrawn before the realisation of heat occurs. Inhalation of any material causes reflex coughing. The pupil of the eye opens and closes in response to the amount of light entering the eye.

Association centres

Certain areas of the brain are supplied with fibres from all the

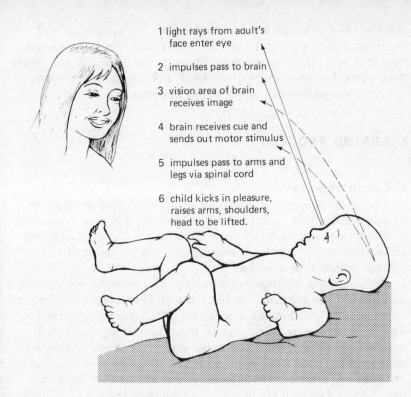

1 light rays from adult's face enter eye

2 impulses pass to brain

3 vision area of brain receives image

4 brain receives cue and sends out motor stimulus

5 impulses pass to arms and legs via spinal cord

6 child kicks in pleasure, raises arms, shoulders, head to be lifted.

Fig 11.2   brain activity involved in anticipation of being lifted

principal sense centres of sight, hearing, smell, taste, touch, and enable several impulses to be co-ordinated.

Association centres plus 'stored' experience allow reflexes to be conditioned (see p. 126) and other forms of learning to take place.

LEARNING

How do we learn? Exactly how is not clear. Emotional security is important for learning and adult encouragement provides motivation. Several processes are involved and language plays a very great part.

During the first 2–3 years of life, when there is rapid increase in the size and number of nerve fibres and myelination is progressing, learning is extensive in spite of limited language. Early evidence of learning is the excitement shown by a baby who hears the sounds of food being prepared. He has learnt to discriminate between different sounds and associated some sounds with parts of his daily care e.g. feeding. Later, but before 1 year

125

old, the child will look for a discarded toy. The permanence of an object out of sight has been learned. Given one brick, he will hold that and accept a second. Offered a 3rd brick, he will pause for a second in time, discard one brick and accept the new one.

Every new experience is a learning opportunity.

LEARNING PROCESS

1 Conditioned reflex

Conditioning is a method whereby an action occurs in response to a stimulus which is not the natural or expected one. It involves a form of learning based on experience and is therefore acquired rather than innate. Unlike a reflex action, the conditioned reflex can be 'unlearnt' or 'modified'.

Many mothers practise 'conditioning' in the early potty practice they provide for the baby. At birth, the child empties his bowel by reflex action. The stimulus is a feeling of fullness in the bowel due to stretching by faecal matter, the response is relaxation of the anal sphincter muscle and expulsion of the waste matter. By observing the baby's excretion pattern, and sitting him on a pot at the time when bowel action is likely, the mother can condition the child to evacuate his bowel when he feels the rim of the pot on his buttocks.

Gradually, with maturity, voluntary control suppresses this reflex action. This is not a primitive reflex that goes away, as grasping and walking reflexes do, but one that remains only to return when voluntary control is lost due to brain damage, unconsciousness or nerve damage.

2 Association

Within the 1st year we see evidence of the baby making associations between objects. He will rattle a spoon in a cup, attempt to brush his hair. Similarly, he learns to associate voices with people and words with objects. These are usually words and objects that are familiar and in common usage in his daily life. It is this process of association which aids the early development of language and concept formation, and he clearly demonstrates his ability to understand more than he can say.

3 Imitation

Much of the early learning of babyhood, and later, takes place by imitation. It is very pleasing for a mother to see her baby attempting to wash himself, lift a telephone and hold it to his ear,

Fig 11.3   '...learning by imitation.'

play pat-a-cake, use a simple posting box, in response to being shown.

Language is, of course, the skill which most easily demonstrates learning by imitation. When we consider the importance of learning by imitation, we realise how necessary it is that the child has a good model to copy. As well as language, many of the child's social skills are acquired in this way e.g. feeding, dressing, behaviour. It is also by imitation that some emotional control is learned. Habits, desirable or otherwise, may also be learnt by imitation.

4 Modelling
This is a rather special kind of imitation, typified by a child using someone else as an example of how to behave. During childhood, and later, modelling is a method used to understand a role. Early role play shows children experimenting with how it feels to be a parent, a nurse, a doctor, a bus conductor, a lorry driver.

5 Learning by doing (direct experience)
It is not just in childhood that we learn most easily by doing, but· in childhood when experience is just beginning the child needs the opportunity to explore his world and experience situations in a

Fig 11.4 modelling

sensory and physical way. Largely, he learns by trial and error, by discovery, by being presented with different materials and situations. His learning will be enhanced and expanded by the adult who discusses with him what he is doing, suggests alternatives, opens other doors to exploration: an adult who uses different words to describe the same thing, and expands his vocabulary.

Structured play for children is based on the theory that learning takes place by doing, and the aware adult will always make the child's environment stimulating and provide encouragement and praise as incentives to learn.

Children (like adults) learn from their mistakes, but the sensitive adult will ensure that successes occur too, otherwise frustration will ensue.

6 Reinforcement

A child's behaviour may be moulded by a process of reinforcement. In simple terms, this means the child is rewarded or punished according to the view taken of his conduct. Reward may be simple, 'Well done. Good boy.' Punishment may be a stern look or a strong word. Reward and punishment are different things to different people and different things to the same person in various circumstances.

Punishment should be reserved for really important issues. Guidance is usually a better alternative. Encouragement builds confidence and therefore makes learning pleasurable.

Fig 11.5   direct experience

INTELLECTUAL DEVELOPMENT

What does this mean? Development of the mind; the acquisition of knowledge. The anatomical and physiological developments that bring about learning are not precisely known. We do know that all areas of development are closely inter-related. So closely related, in fact, that no one area will progress successfully without comparable development in all other areas. For example, a child with defective speech organs has difficulty with his social and intellectual development. As a result, his emotional development may be affected. The child who lacks mobility relies on others to provide him with experiences. He must be transported or experiences must be brought to him. Learning for this child is, therefore, dependent upon the insight and goodwill of others. An alert mind in a handicapped body must suffer all kinds of frustration and result in social and emotional problems. Similarly, a handicapped mind or personality may affect physical performance.

The only guide to the developing intellect of a small baby is what he shows us in a physical way: his posture, the level of maturity he shows when he moves, sits, stands; his developing manipulative skill and language; the manner in which he expresses emotion and responds socially.

Physical prowess is demonstrated in large motor activity and the co-ordination that makes it purposeful. Walking development, running, skipping, hopping, balance, climbing all indicate a stage of physical development. Combine manipulative skill with this and the child can ride a bicycle, scoot, turn a skipping rope, destroy and construct. Is this purely physical skill? No, these activities require brain growth, nervous maturation, quick reflexes, problem solving ability. A child will only succeed at these skills if he has also developed the patience to try again when he fails. Developing orientation, balance, and depth perception increase an awareness of the relationship between his body and the world around him.

Growth may take place with good nutrition and care, but it is not possible to divorce any aspects of child development from brain activity. The brain is the command centre for all human function. Mobility, vision and fine skill, hearing and communication, sociability, emotional and moral development are all dependent upon healthy brain function.

Practice of developing skills is of paramount importance if learning is to take place. This importance is evident in the play of a young child, who will repeat and repeat an activity almost as if he instinctively knows what is necessary for his own intellectual development.

The toddler who climbs the ladder of a slide for the 1st time and successfully descends will go again and again and again. He seems to be perfecting the skill and gaining confidence each time An important motivation is the adult who laughs with him and shares his enjoyment. With no-one to watch and encourage, he is likely to give up sooner.

The next leap forward in learning comes with the spurt in language development during the 2nd and 3rd years of life. It is evident from the toddler's behaviour that his mechanisms for storin and remembering information develop before he can reproduce th sounds he hears. Very soon his babbling takes on recognisable sounds within his own language and words become associated with objects. As connections continue to form between centres o understanding and centres of vision and hearing, so vocabulary expands and concepts are built.

Assessment of intellectual development becomes easier as language develops. The ways in which a child uses language to express his desires, his thoughts, his feelings, give us some

'Be careful, the iron's hot!'

'It's not too hot to drink.'

'Don't go near the fire — it's hot!'

'I'm hot!'

'The sun's hot today.'

Fig 11.6   concept formation (a combination of experience and language) e.g. 'HOT'

indication of memory, reasoning, problem solving ability and personality traits.

As with motor and fine skills, practice at language and repetition have a great part to play. Repetitive rhymes and jingles are great favourites and a source of fun. Little children can be heard playing with new words that seem to hold a fascination for them. They are used over and over again until the child has become familiar with their use. By trial and error, and with guidance, he learns when to and when not to use the word.

In our care of young children we must always pay attention to the fact that hereditary endowment may limit potential, but the environment in which the child grows up will determine the extent to which that potential is exploited. Adults have a responsibility to bring into a child's life as many varied experiences as possible, to answer questions, to explain, to engage him in conversation and to use all practical incentives to motivate learning.

Praise encourages achievement. Success breeds success.

12
Play

THE PURPOSE OF PLAY

Over the years, there have been many theories put forward about play. It has been said at different times by different people that play is a means of letting off superfluous energy; it is instinctive preparation for adult life; it is relaxation from the stresses of living; it is the expression of what a child thinks and feels. Possibly, play is all of these.

Through play the young child learns as many physical, social and intellectual skills as his hereditary endowment and environment

Fig 12.1   domestic play — creative, imaginative, imitative, solitary and adventurous

will allow and, at the same time, develops emotional control. At play, the child learns control of his limbs and body, develops balance and co-ordination. Through play he explores, reasons, makes judgements and develops problem solving techniques. Through play a child establishes emotional balance, he becomes a social being who can share, co-operate and show respect for others. Play is fun.

Types of play can be classified, but seldom separated. It is possible to observe creative play, imaginative play, co-operative play, pretend play, imitative play, physical play, solitary play, group play, domestic play, adventurous play etc. In many instances, a child will indulge in 2 or 3 of these types of play simultaneously.

Classification and philosophising are academic exercises of little value unless this practice leads the adult to consider the materials, opportunities and experiences offered to the playing child.

THE VALUE OF PLAY

Play has been a characteristic of childhood for centuries, but it is only in relatively recent years that the play in which children indulge has been seen to have any value. Even now, some adults have to be convinced of the role that play has in the healthy development of children.

This may be due to the fact that some view play in the light of the flippancy of adult play! There is an ambiguity between play for the adult and play for the child. Adult 'play' is an acceptable reward after work. How do we interpret play as far as children are concerned? Possibly there are 2 answers to this question. We can validate play in terms of its relationship with normal development. This is spontaneous play, that is derived from the innate desire to be active and a curiosity instinct. Children's play can also be viewed in terms of its therapeutic or diagnostic values. Here, the play situation is often engineered in order to demonstrate facets of the child's abilities or behaviour. The sensitive observer may make judgements about the stage of development the child has reached and therefore decide the course of action in the future.

Play presents the child with many learning opportunities essential to wholesome development. Play makes contributions to the development of a child, most of which cannot be made through other channels. Play for children has begun to have status and now less frequently we hear, 'He's only playing'.

Physical value

Vigorous play is essential if the young child is to develop strength and tone in his muscles and exercise all parts of his body. At the same time, he is practising nervous co-ordination and quick responses.

In early motor development, learning to control the large muscles and total body movements help the child to overcome some of his frustrations. Mobility allows a child to channel the energy generated by frustration in more constructive ways. Fine skills allow the child to achieve independence and self reliance.

Emotional value
Play allows a child to release pent up emotions in useful ways. He can work through aggression with clay and dough, he can come to terms with anxiety, fear and jealousy in dramatic play. Role play will allow the child who seeks status to become a leader for a short while, to practise other social roles.

Educational value
By exploring the properties of all types of materials, he learns how they feel, how they behave and what he can do with them. He comes to terms with his environment and discovers his strengths and weaknesses, his powers and his restrictions. He develops an awareness of danger.

Exploring, collecting and talking about these collections will teach him much, long before he can read. In his play, the child builds a picture of himself (self concept). Experimentation allows him to test his developing skills without taking full responsibility for his actions. He can make mistakes safely and discover cause and effect. Play stimulates thought, reasoning, problem solving skills, all of which he brings to bear on his play and so extends the experience.

Social value
In the early days of babyhood, play has a social value at mother distance. Later, he will learn to make relationships with strangers, both children and adults, and develop social skills to overcome the demands of any relationship. Through play, he learns to give and take, to win and lose.

Moral value
Fairness, honesty, truthfulness, self control are all qualities that can develop through play. In play situations he learns that he must conform to certain rules in order to be accepted.

Diagnostic value
Doctors, **psychologists**, educational psychologists, **speech therapists**, physiotherapists, health visitors and teachers all

use a child's ability to play as a yardstick by which to assess development. In the diagnostic situation, several meaningful questions must be answered. Does the child play at all? With what does he play? How does he play? What skills are demonstrated while he plays? Does he play alone? Does he play with adults? Does he play with other children? How long does he play? Is his play varied? How does he use language in play situations?

In order to answer these questions, the observer will structure the play experiences offered to the child. The results observed will enable the professional person to recommend a course of action.

Fun value

Last, but not least, play should bring enjoyment, encourage laughter and a sense of humour. The 'fun value' is very evident in the spontaneous play of the young baby who coos and gurgles with delight at the peek-a-boo games, the tickles and caresses that accompany his play. Listen to the laughter and exclamations of pleasure that can be heard in a playroom or playground. Hopefully, the pendulum will not now swing to the extreme that play is taken so seriously that the 'fun' element is lost.

PATTERN OF PLAY DEVELOPMENT

Play is related to development. The baby's first play materials are himself and his mother. He engages in random large movements, which become more purposeful as control develops. He clasps and unclasps his hands, he pats the breast or bottle when he feeds. He brings objects to his mouth for exploration and his early play materials must be chosen with this in mind.

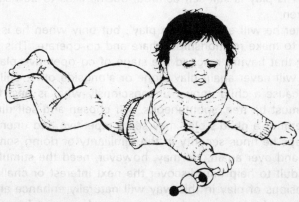

Fig 12.2   solitary play

Fig 12.3   parallel play

At this early stage, his play develops muscle tone, posture and mobility. Simultaneously, he practises hand/eye co-ordination. He explores his senses and engages in visual, auditory and tactile experiments. Each rewarding experience encourages its practice and therefore perfection in the skill.

This is the period of solitary play. He is happy to play alone but demands and enjoys social and tactile responses of his favourite adults.

The confidence that comes from this enjoyment leads him to 'parallel play'. This is the stage at which the young child (2–3 years) will play alongside other children but not in a co-operative way. His play is still self centred, but he likes to be near other children.

Later he will enjoy 'group play', but only when he is ready to learn to make relationships, share and co-operate. This does not imply that having reached the stage of co-operative play that a child will never again play alone or alongside other children.

Because a child knows unconsciously what is best for him, his play must be free, spontaneous, self chosen and self directed. Sometimes a child's play may seem repetitive and unenterprising. Perhaps he finds security in the familiarity of doing something over and over again. He may, however, need the stimulations of the adult to help him discover the next interest or challenge. Extensions of play in this way will naturally enhance and be enhanced by language development and concept formation.

Fig 12.4   learning to make relationships, share and co-operate

PLAY IN RELATION TO DEVELOPMENT AND LEARNING

A baby's brain is extremely receptive to sensory experience. As well as physical care and great attention paid to emotional security, the caring adult should fill the baby's waking hours with gentle stimulation to touch, sight, smell, taste, hearing. In the early days, much of this experience occurs at the breast. His mother's scent, her feel, her taste are all experienced when he roots at the breast for the nipple and fixes upon it to suck. As already mentioned, he will demand visual attention when feeding and, if this need is met, he will respond by feeding contentedly. If his mother speaks soothing encouraging words too, his sensory world is complete — for the moment!

Fig 12.5   'His mother's scent, her feel, her taste ...'

Very soon, within the 1st weeks of life, his world begins to expand and already he makes preliminary experiments in an attempt to understand the world around him. As wakeful periods become prolonged, he raises his head, looks around and listens, he clasps and unclasps his hands exploring the possibilities of those parts of his body that are within reach. Often by accident at this stage, his clothing or toes will come into his grasp and these are brought to his mouth for exploration.

Already he is responding differently to different sounds. It is not so much a case of what is said to him, rather the tone in which it is expressed. A favourite human voice will elicit a degree of excitement, it has special meaning; the vacuum cleaner or telephone, on the other hand, causes a response of awareness and an alert expression but seldom produces the excited response that results from 'human' sounds. Music appears to have special significance. Perhaps even in these early days, he is discriminating and committing to memory some of the wealth of sound that the world offers him.

Some of the crying seen in very young babies can be attributed to boredom. In a busy world, adults cannot always be present and at this stage of development some other form of visual or aural stimulation will keep him happy. A mobile, washing blowing in the wind, the movement of trees, the sound of traffic, music, general household noise will satisfy him temporarily, but nothing is a substitute for human company, and particularly human talk. It is never too early to talk to a baby.

At this stage, he needs a variety of objects and play materials to touch: water to splash, paper that rustles and paper that doesn't, rattles, 'banging toys', saucepans, wooden spoons and plastic cartons. This variety will often provide him with visual and aural experience, too. In most kitchens a child will find a selection of household objects which will aid his hand/eye co-ordination and provide a wealth of sensory experience. Sophisticated toys are unnecessary at this time.

Colour is important. Bright colours appeal to all babies and serve to attract attention. It will be some time before colour discrimination occurs, but a brightly coloured object is an incentive to move towards it, and to explore it, once having made contact.

Safety is always a factor to be considered in every aspect of care, but particularly so in the choice of objects given to him to explore independently. For several months, well into the 3rd year and often later, the mouth is used for 'touch' experience.

When the child achieves independent mobility, the house becomes an exciting place. Together with increasing manipulative skill, this ability to move brings him into a world of stairs, steps, doors to be opened, insides and outsides, tops and bottoms, under and overs. 'No' brings learning of what may not be done, but its over-use will inhibit the natural curiosity found in healthy children and it must therefore be saved for important occasions.

From now on, language will aid his learning in all kinds of ways. At first, he uses nouns singly to indicate objects. His desire for those objects is demonstrated by gesture, facial expression and repetition of the word until his needs are met. The curiosity drive with which healthy children appear to be born is the motivation to much of their learning. It is difficult, if not impossible, to be curious about things that quickly become familiar. Therefore, his environment must contain enough of the familiar to maintain security, but must also be changing, dynamic and filled with as many varied and new experiences as possible.

When alone, he can be heard using familiar nouns and verbs to commentate on what he is doing. An attentive, but not intrusive adult can provide him with an increasing number of other words that he will need. Gradually, these are internalised, used and practised to understand his play, to relate what he has done, to anticipate what will happen, to ask questions. He thinks aloud, he thinks in words and gradually abstract concepts are built up.

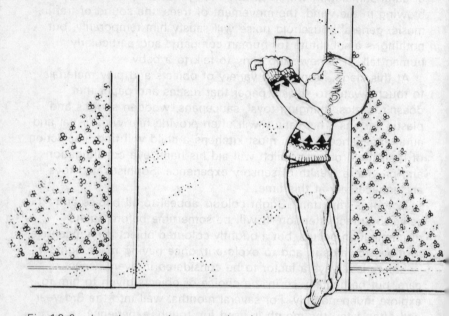

Fig 12.6 '... doors to be opened ...'

In play, he demonstrates a willingness to be social. Faced with a new situation he becomes an observer, later he joins the group to work alongside, but it will be some time before he understands the rules of co-operation, sharing, taking turns and can partake in true group play. To achieve this degree of sociability, he must have gained considerable physical control and an acceptable level of emotional control: acceptable, that is, to his peers who will not make the same allowances for his lapses as would the more tolerant adult.

He is beginning to gain control over his body function and satisfy some of his own needs. He can feed himself, pull off clothing, make attempts at hygiene routines like brushing his hair and cleaning teeth. He is a doer, and now his body will take him where he wants to go and his limbs will do what he wants them to do. This is a time of transition from helpless baby to the onset of individuality and growing independence. Assertion of new found independence can lead to potential conflicts. At times, he will become a baby again, wanting to be fed, to be comforted, to suck his thumb. At other times, he will forcibly resist help and demand self reliance.

His thought processes and language forge ahead and he appears to be happy in his egocentric world. This leads to a willingness to be left alone for short periods, as long as there is an adult to rescue him when he cannot cope, who takes an interest in his achievements and encourages the next step, an adult who smooths away the hurt when he oversteps his abilities.

Gradually, he becomes aware that the world does not entirely revolve around him. His involvement in himself must give way to an awareness of others. 'Wants' cannot always be satisfied immediately. Adults are beginning to explain — 'When I have finished ...', 'After tea ...' and the concept of time is being introduced.

As the socialisation process progresses, he finds himself drawn to small groups who seem to be doing what he would like to do. He may make abortive attempts to join in and fail. That is when the help of the adult will ease the stress and help him to integrate. His greatest obstacle to successful play relationships is often his strong awareness of 'me' and 'mine', but less acceptance of 'you' and 'yours'.

However, periods of concentration are lengthening, vocabulary is expanding and in plenty of time for school he develops a considerable degree of fine skill, sociability, emotional control and body control. These will ease his passage from the security of home and perhaps part time attendance at nursery school or playgroup to the larger, less intimate life of school. Four year olds are great questioners. 'Who?' and 'What?' has been his line of inquiry so far. Now he wants to know 'Why?' and 'How?'

Until now he has been organising himself in many ways, physically, emotionally and socially. Now his intellectual and personality development will lead him to an awareness of himself as a person and the uniqueness of his personality. He tests out his newly acquired skills and develops them further.

Pre-school education should provide him with a safe environment in which he is stimulated to expand his knowledge, practise his language and social skills, help him towards emotional stability, and develop all his physical skills. Falls and stumbling are less frequent now. He can steer and ride a bicycle, balance, climb up and down with confidence, kick, throw and catch a ball. He can change direction in a more confined space, he can charge about with less chance of crashing into other people. His bowel and bladder are controlled, except for rare accidents, and he has accepted greater responsibility for his own care than before.

Imagination is developing, although discrimination between fact and fantasy will not become truly developed for another 3–4 years. Conversation, stories, rhymes, music and all creative activities stimulate his imagination and soon he will be relating long stories himself. Stories that are a collection of short sentences strung together by 'and ... and ... and'. He will use and have an idea of the meaning of circle, rectangle, square, soon, after, before, thin, thick, shallow, deep, light, heavy etc: all important concepts if he is to come to terms with his world and explore its possibilities.

The point at which all aspects of growth and development meet is seen in the play of a young child.

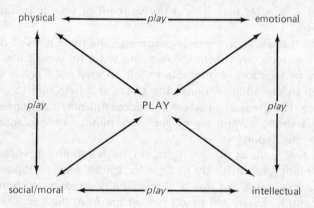

Fig 12.7   play

PLAY IN THE DEVELOPMENT OF READING, WRITING AND NUMERACY

Reading

Reading, a process of decoding, requires the acceptance of symbols as an alternative to words used verbally. Any activity that helps a child to make the connection between the spoken word and the written word is beneficial.

In baby days, an interest in books is shown in a physical way. Board books have pages thick enough for little fingers to turn and colourful pictures provide an incentive to explore further.

Otherwise, the value of board books is debatable. Perhaps they are considered suitable for the young baby because they withstand sucking longer than the paper variety!

The motivation to read comes largely from the intimate moments experienced on the adult's knee, when objects in pictures are named, stories are read, and verse is shared. From these secure, pleasurable moments comes increasing conversation, expanded vocabulary and the ability to listen.

Fig 12.8   '... most valuable contribution to reading ...'

Discrimination of size and shape are especially important skills to be acquired and these can be encouraged by activities that involve sorting and matching e.g. posting boxes, picture card games and jigsaws.

In order to read successfully, a child must be taught the 'direction of reading'. In western cultures, the left to right and top to bottom arrangement of words must be followed. Long before the reading of words is possible, this flow can be encouraged by picture books with no text, and comics.

A child with an adequate vocabulary will soon make up his own stories to pictures that depict everyday happenings within his

143

experience. When simple text is introduced, pictures continue to give clues to words contained in the print. As a book becomes familiar, the desire to read is demonstrated by the child who points to words, recites remembered phrases and exclaims, 'I'm reading!'

Whilst any caring adult can encourage a love of books and show their potential, many teachers believe that the teaching of reading should be left to the experts. This view does not deny the most valuable contribution to reading made by parents, pre-school playgroup helpers, nursery staff and others, but rather emphasises the skill of the professional in recognising the difficulties of individual children. However, there is no disagreement about the importance of adult help. No child will come to reading on his own any more than he will come to speak a language to which he is not exposed.

Pre-writing skills

From the earliest days, when the feeding baby pats the breast or bottle, explores his fingers and toes, reaches towards a colourful toy, he is preparing for writing and other fine skills. Any play that involves the use of fingers and the co-ordination of hands and

Fig 12.9 '... painting ... develops ... fine manipulative skill.'

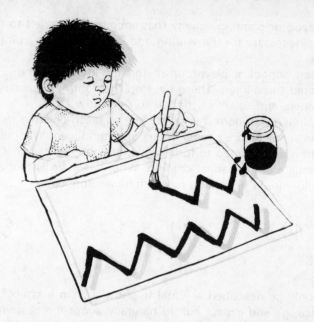

Fig 12.10   'painting ... encourages the left to right movement ...'

eyes is excellent practice, too. Which hand becomes favourite is unimportant. Left to his own devices, the young child will experiment with each hand, and quite unconsciously adopt one for preference (handedness).

When the adult places a spoon in the hand of the child for the 1st time, he/she is helping the child towards writing skills. Painting, first with hands and fingers, and later with brushes and painting materials, develops further the manipulative skill.

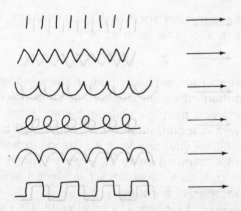

Fig 12.11   examples of rhythmic patterns

Any crayon or painting activity that encourages the left to right movement necessary for the writing adopted by western cultures is of value.

At nursery school or playgroup rhythmic patterns will be demonstrated to children. These develop the control necessary for forming letters and establish the left to right flow.

In the United Kingdom it is customary to teach children to use lower case script before capital letters are introduced. Whether or not a child is encouraged to form his letters on lined paper is open to debate and personal opinion. What is certain is that a young child should be shown how letters are formed.

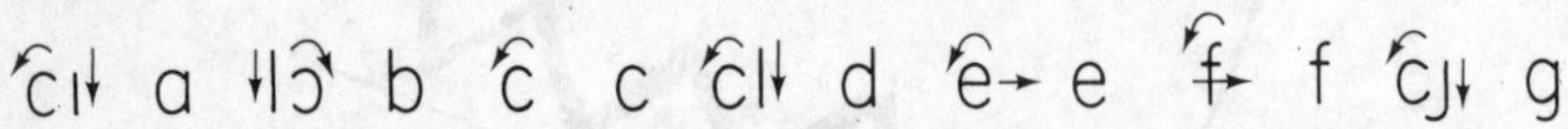

€I⏐ a ⏐⏋ b ĉ c Ĉ⏐ d ê→ e ꟷ꜀ f ꞔⱼ⏐ g

Fig 12.12

It can only be described as cruel to show a child a symbol, for instance 'g', and expect him to naturally adopt the customary method of forming that symbol. Individuality in style of writing will develop later, but in these early stages he needs help. Writing is an art form, used for communication. Illegible writing is not only valueless as a means of communication, it can be an irritation. If a child is to derive pleasure from acceptable writing, the mystique must be eradicated and the activity must be enjoyable.

In order that the association between what he reads and what he writes may be made most easily, it is helpful if all adults who help him adopt the same style, and the writing he learns corresponds as closely as possible with the printing he finds in his first reading books.

Minor variations in form are relatively unimportant, but is 'y' the same as '*y*'; is 'k' the same letter as '*k*'?

Numeracy

Concepts of number are gradually built in the mind of a young child, largely through their introduction, use and practice. Number vocabulary starts very early with simple games. From the time the baby can eat with a spoon, the meal is encouraged by phrases like 'one spoonful for you, one for me'. Going up and down stairs often made into a counting game. Rhymes and jingles help the process along: 'One, two, three, four, five, once I caught a fish alive'; 'One, two, buckle my shoe'.

In the first stages of language, a small child will use 'number words' long before he understands the 'oneness of one'. He will

Fig 12.13 '... numeracy must first be experienced physically.'

'count' to 10 long before he understands numerical order. As well as mathematical vocabulary and concepts of number, the child must learn that each number is characterised by a symbol.

Building, sorting, matching, the making of sets, are all valuable experience for the foundation of numeracy. Sand, water, dough, clay all provide the opportunity for the adult to introduce and give the child experience of 'more than', 'less than', 'wider than', 'shorter than' etc.

As with many other forms of learning, numeracy must first be experienced physically. Two bricks must be handled, built, knocked down. Three oranges must be seen to have a similar quality to 3 apples, 3 plums, 3 cherries.

Enjoyable practice are the key words for early skills.

Conclusion

For ease of learning, it is helpful for students of child development to consider aspects of development separately, but they must never lose sight of the 'whole child' — this small being, in whom all areas of development are progressing simultaneously and harmoniously.

What does harmonious progression imply? Simply, it means that a child is passing through the patterns of development in his own time but within acceptable limits of 'normality'.

Throughout this book, rarely has reference been made to age and stage, or milestones. This was deliberate because it is only in developmental assessment that developmental norms are used by the paediatrician, psychologist, health visitor or teacher. Most students of child development must be aware of the progress of growth and development in order to cater for children's needs and to be able to report accurately to these professionals information which may aid the assessment.

Growth can be measured with a degree of accuracy in terms of weight, height and proportion. Development can only be assessed and is therefore open to variability and personal interpretation.

Developmental assessment and the decision of 'normality' or otherwise must, therefore, be left to the specialists who are not only equipped by years of training and experience to make such an important judgement, but are also in a position to advise parents and mobilise any resources necessary to assist the child who needs special help.

This book is an introduction to child development. It is hoped that the information contained here will tempt the appetite and lead to further reading in this absorbing subject.

Glossary

abortion ejection of the foetus before the 28th week of pregnancy.

adenoids spongy tissue between the back of the nose and throat.

adolescence that period between the onset of puberty and adulthood.

ammonia a colourless mixture of nitrogen and hydrogen, with a sharp smell and strong alkaline reaction.

amnion inner membrane enclosing the foetus.

amniotic fluid liquid substance contained within the amnion.

anaemia lack of red blood cells or haemoglobin, resulting in pale skin colouring.

antibodies chemical substances in the blood which have protective properties.

anxiety condition of agitation and apprehension; fear of what has happened or what might happen.

atrophy emaciation; decrease in size or wasting away through imperfect nourishment.

auditory nerve the bundle of fibres concerned with transmitting sound to the brain.

bilirubin a reddish pigment in bile which is a fluid excreted by the liver to aid the digestive process.

binocular vision seeing the same object with both eyes simultaneously.

breech presentation the lower half of the baby's body is the part that leads down the birth canal.

Caesarian section surgical operation to remove the baby from the uterus through the abdomen. (Caesar is said to have been delivered this way.)

changing stool greenish faeces that begin to form once feeding is started.

chorion outer membrane covering the foetus.

chromosomes determinants of heredity found in cell nucleus.

cleft palate a defect, leaving a longitudinal gap in the roof of the mouth, sometimes resulting in speech problems later.

cochlea spiral cavity in the ear, concerned with receiving sound.

colostrum nutritious substance produced by the breasts before the true milk.

colour blindness a defect among males who have inherited a recessive gene from their mothers and are unable to distinguish some or all of the colours of the spectrum.

concept formation understanding an abstract notion; forming a general idea or thought.

conception union of the male sperm and the female ovum.

convergence inward turning of the eyes to fix on an object.

cornea transparent front covering of the eyeball.

culture trait, belief, custom; practices associated with a social group.

cystic fibrosis congenital condition causing deposits of tough fibrous tissue in, for example, the pancreas and lungs.

depression low spirits, dejection; a feeling of sadness and hopelessness.

depth perception perceiving depth or distance.

diabetic one who suffers from diabetes mellitus, a disorder causing inability to control sugars in the body.

diaphysis shaft of a long bone, as distinct from the ends.

ectoderm external germinal layer of the embryo.

embryo developing human in the womb between the 3rd and 8th weeks after conception.

emotion expression of mood; a mental state.

endoderm inner layer of cells in skin.

enzyme complex organic substance which brings about chemical changes in the body e.g. digestion.

epidermis thin layer of skin, or cuticle, forming an external protective covering for the skin.

epiphyses any portion of a bone having its own centre of ossification.

ergosterol substance contained in the skin which in the presence of ultra-violet light is capable of making vitamin D.

Eustachian tube small canal connecting the middle ear with the throat and stabilising air pressure in the middle ear.

factors conditions and influences that act with others to bring about a result.

fibroids swellings in the uterus caused by diseased cells dividing and increasing.

foetus the developing human between the 9th week after conception and birth.

fontanelles areas of membrane covering the brain.

forceps delivery an assisted birth: forceps are applied to the baby to facilitate his passage through the birth canal.

genes hereditary material found in chromosomes. Each gene controls the development of one or more quality or characteristic which has been passed on from the parents.

genitalia the external reproductive organs.

gonorrhoea a venereal disease of the sex organs, causing an inflammatory discharge of pus.

haemoglobin substance in the blood capable of combining with oxygen to carry it round the body.

haemophilia a congenital condition prevalent in boys characterised by the inability of the blood to clot.

handedness the tendency to use one hand predominantly.

hernia a tumour caused by the walls of internal organs being ruptured.

jaundice a disease causing yellowness of the skin, fluids and tissues, constipation and a loss of appetite.

kibbutzim communal agricultural settlements (*kibbutz* in the singular).

lactation the production of milk for babies by the mother, and the time it lasts.

lymphocytes special white cells in blood which are important in the production of antibodies to fight infection.

maturity the state of being complete in natural development; fully grown and with well developed mental and emotional faculties.

meconium a collection of waste products which accumulate in the bowels during pre-natal life.

mesoderm the middle layer of tissues in skin.

moulding the overriding of skull bones.

mutation a genetic change, transmitted to the offspring, producing a variation.

nucleus command centre of a cell containing chromosomes.

obstetrician a specialist in the conduct of pregnancy, delivery and post-natal care.

onomatopoeic adjective describing the formation of a word in imitation of the sound of the thing meant e.g. 'bow wow' for dog.

optic nerve the fibres concerned with transmitting visual stimuli to the brain.

orthodontist a specialist who rectifies dental abnormalities.

oscilloscope electrical equipment that will record and display on a screen impulses received.

ossicles 3 small bones in the middle ear concerned with the conduction of sound.

oviduct the tube through which the ovum passes from the ovary to the womb.

paediatricians doctors who specialise in children's development and illnesses.

patency the state of being open, passage unobstructed.

peer group contemporaries, equal in rank.

pepsin an enzyme contained in gastric juice which, in the presence of a weak acid, converts proteins into peptones.

peristalsis rippling muscle action found in the alimentary tract.

phenylketonuria a severe form of mental deficiency, resulting from the baby's inability to metabolise phenylalanine. If it is diagnosed soon after birth, and the infant is given a diet low in phenylalanine, the child may well grow up mentally normal.

placenta the structure which provides nourishment to the foetus. It also acts as a barrier to infection.

poliomyelitis inflammation of the nerves in the backbone often resulting in a lasting inability to move certain muscles (paralysis).

prematurity born before the completion of the gestation period.

psychologists specialists in human behaviour.

pulmonary pertaining to or relating to the lungs.

puréed reduced (food material) to a pulp.

quickening the stage in pregnancy when the mother becomes conscious of the movements of the child.

radiation energy transmitted in electro-magnetic waves.

recessive gene a characteristic suppressed by a more dominant one.

reflex actions unlearned, involuntary responses to some outside influence(s).

retina innermost, light sensitive part of the eye.

sebum oily substance, produced in the sebaceous glands, that lubricates the hair and skin.

semi-circular canals part of the inner ear concerned with balance.

sesamoid a small, rounded bone in the substance of a tendon.

siblings children who have one or both parents in common.

sinus an abscess, or sore, forming a narrow, hollow cavity in bone tissue.

speech therapists specialists trained to help people with various kinds of difficulties to speak plainly.

subcutaneous lying or situated under the skin.

suspensory ligament tissue supporting the lens of the eye.

sutures junctions of 2 or more bones in the skull.

syphilis a serious venereal disease which can be passed on during sexual activity or from parent to child. The infection is caused by an organism, the spirochaete of syphilis.

tonsils 2 small, roundish organs at the sides of the throat near the back of the tongue.

tuberculosis a serious disease that affects many parts of the body, in particular the lungs.

umbilical cord tube which carries nutrition to the foetus and returns waste products to the mother for excretion.

venereal diseases those infections transmitted by means of sexual contact. Derived from Venus, the goddess of love.

ventouse extraction delivery of the baby by suction.

ventral suspension the holding of the child, face down, by supporting the chest. This enables the observer to see the degree of head control and the natural posture assumed by arms and legs.

whooping cough a disease, usually caught by children, in which each bout of coughing is followed by a long noisy intake of breath.

Suggested further reading

Berg, L. (1972) *Look at Kids*. Penguin

Bilski, A. (1977) *The Vital Years and Your Child*. Souvenir Press

Bower, T. G. (1977) *The Perceptual World of the Child*. Fontana

Brierley, J. (1976) *The Growing Brain: Childhood's Crucial Years*. National Foundation for Educational Research

Bronowski, J. (1976) *The Ascent of Man*. B B C Publications

Cass, J. E. (1973) *Helping Children Grow Through Play*. Schocken

Cass, J. E. (1971) *The Significance of Children's Play*. Batsford

Donaldson, M. (1978) *Children's Minds*. Fontana/Collins

Gessell, A. *et al.* (1971) *The First Five Years of Life*. Methuen

Green, R. T. and Laxon, V. J. (1978) *Entering the World of Number*. Thames & Hudson

Gunther, M. (1970) *Infant Feeding*. Methuen

Hurlock, E. (1973) *Child Development*. McGraw Hill

Hurlock, E. (1970) *Child Growth and Development*. McGraw Hill.

Illingworth, R. S. and C. M. (1977) *Babies and Young Children*. Churchill Livingstone

Jackson, B. (1979) *Starting School*. Coom Helm, London

Jameson, K. and Kidd, P. (1974) *Pre-school Play*. Studio Vista

Kitzinger, S. (1978) *Women as Mothers*. Martin Robertson in association with Fontana

Lewis, D. (1978) *The Secret Language of Your Child*. Souvenir Press

Lowenfeld, V. and Brittan, W. L. (1975) *Creative and Mental Growth*. Collier Macmillan

Lucas, J. and V. (1974) *The Penguin Book of Playgroups*. Penguin

Nilsson, L. (1977) *A Child Is Born*. Faber

Pringle, M. K. (1975) *The Needs of Children*. Hutchinson

Roberts, V. (1971) *Play, Learning and Living*. A. & C. Black

Sheridan, M. D. (1973) *Children's Developmental Progress from Birth to Five Years*. National Foundation for Educational Research

Tough, J. (1977) *The Development of Meaning: A Study of Children's Use of Language*. Allen & Unwin

Tough, J. (1974) *Focus on Meaning.* Allen & Unwin
Tough, J. (1976) *Listening to Children Talking.* Ward Lock
Tough, J. (1978) *Talking and Learning.* Ward Lock
Tucker, N. (1977) *What Is a Child?* Fontana
Vulliamy, D. G. (1977) *The Newborn Child.* Churchill Livingstone
Willis, M. and McLachlan, M. E. (1977) *Medical Care in Schools.*
    E. Arnold

Index